How to Design & Build Sheds

Created and Designed by the Editorial Staff of Ortho Books

Editors
Robert J. Beckstrom
Sally W. Smith

Writer
Paul Ehrlich

Shed Plans By
Joe Bologna
Paul Ehrlich

Illustrator
Tony Davis

Ortho Books

Publisher
Robert B. Loperena

Editorial Director
Christine Jordan

Manufacturing Director
Ernie S. Tasaki

Managing Editor
Sally W. Smith

Editors
Robert J. Beckstrom
Michael D. Smith

Prepress Supervisor
Linda M. Bouchard

Sales & Marketing Manager
David C. José

Publisher's Assistant
Joni Christiansen

Graphics Coordinator
Sally J. French

Editorial Coordinator
Cass Dempsey

Copyeditor
Barbara Feller-Roth

Proofreader
Alicia K. Eckley

Indexer
Trisha Lamb Feuerstein

Separations by
Color Tech Corp.

Lithographed in the USA by
Banta Company

Special Thanks to
Deborah Cowder
David Van Ness
Mike and Marilyn Jensen-
 Akula
Yountville Elementary School

Photographers
Patricia J. Bruno/Positive
 Images: 18–19
Karen Bussolini/Positive
 Images: 8, back cover BL
Barbara J. Ferguson: back
 cover BR
Michael Landis: 11T, 11B
Geoffrey Nilsen: 1
Ortho Photo Library: 3T, 3B,
 12, 80–81
Kenneth Rice: Front cover,
 4–5, 6, 46–47, back cover TR
T. Jeff Williams: 14, back
 cover TL

Designers and Builders
Cynthia Brian, ASID, Starstyle
 Design: 6
Chris E. Hecht Design &
 Landscape Construction
Paul Johnson, The Shed Shop:
 Front cover, 4–5, back
 cover TR
Jason Kaldis, Jarvis Architects:
 46–47
Michael Landis: 11T, 11B

Front Cover
The materials for this Basic Gable-Roofed Shed are readily available at any home center: plywood siding, framing lumber, pier blocks, composition shingles, an aluminum window, hardware, and paint.

Title Page
Why should a garden shed be a boring box? Shed walls offer an opportunity for a degree of whimsy that you'd never attempt on your house.

Page 3
Top: Many shed designs are inspired by architecture from around the world. A few simple details give this garden shed a Japanese flavor.

Bottom: Once your shed is built, you can organize the storage space with some shelves and racks, and a bench.

Back Cover
Top left: Building a simple shed calls for standard construction techniques such as creating a foundation and framing a stud wall.

Top right, bottom left, and bottom right: These sheds—in the basic styles of Gambrel-Roofed, Gable-Roofed, and Lean-to—illustrate the variety possible in outdoor storage structures. Whether you need a shed for the open country-side or for an urban backyard, you can design a structure to fit any available space and to enhance its surroundings.

Address all inquiries to:
Ortho Books
Box 5006
San Ramon, CA 94583-0906

© 1996 Monsanto Company
All rights reserved

1 2 3 4 5 6 7 8 9
96 97 98 99 2000 01

ISBN 0-89721-283-5
Library of Congress Catalog Card
Number 95-68608

Disclaimer
Do not purchase materials or attempt to build any project unless you have studied the plans thoroughly, have verified all dimensions and materials requirements for yourself, and have verified that they conform to local building codes and practices. Although every effort has been made to ensure the accuracy of the information and designs, the reader is ultimately responsible for the use of these plans and descriptions.

These plans are copyrighted and cannot be duplicated without permission of the Publisher, nor any structures built for any purpose except the private use of the reader.

THE SOLARIS GROUP
2527 Camino Ramon
San Ramon, CA 94583-0906

How to Design & Build Sheds

PLANNING FOR SUCCESSFUL STORAGE

Everyone has stuff, the possessions we accumulate over the years. Much of it—bicycles, grills, tools, lawn mowers, gardening equipment, games, sporting equipment, camping gear, hobby supplies—is best stored out of the house, and efficiently: out of sight and protected from the elements yet easily accessible.

This book helps you create such storage. Its main emphasis is on sheds, the most common and most practical solution to outdoor storage needs, but there are also many other ideas for storing things outdoors. The first chapter will get you started, with practical strategies for planning and organizing your outdoor storage, including guidelines for designing a shed. The next chapter presents designs and complete building instructions for four basic sheds. More complex shed designs appear in the following chapter. The final chapter covers storage components and strategies for solving common storage problems; it includes simple designs for building your own racks, shelves, hangers, and other storage devices.

Does everyone in your family grumble when it's time to clean up the yard? They might not find the chore so dreary if they had a convenient shed for storing equipment and supplies. Adding a few details to the shed, such as the trellis, window box, and carriage light seen here, will make it all the more appealing.

PREPARING A PLAN

Planning a successful outdoor storage system involves more than finding new space for more things. It calls for a careful look at your yard and structures, and a thoughtful analysis of what kind of space you need. Use the five-step planning process given here to create your optimum outdoor storage system.

Step 1: Sort Your Things

Planning a storage system starts with evaluating what you are storing. Begin by determining how important each item is to you. All your belongings have value: monetary value, sentimental value, or "use" value.

If an item has monetary value, perhaps it should be in more secure storage. But do you really need it? Consider trading or selling it.

Things with sentimental value are more difficult to relinquish. Think hard about whether they are worth keeping, especially if you are not using them. Perhaps the most caring approach would be giving them to someone who *will* use them. Try to part with at least some items.

Useful things are often the hardest to release—antique chairs that need repair, old or damaged tools, lawn furniture, toys, tires, inner tubes, gardening tools, or assorted supplies such as lumber or nails.

Start by asking yourself if they are genuinely useful. Are you really going to recane that antique chair? Will your grandchildren really want a rusty old tricycle? You'll be surprised at the sense of relief and freedom when you start letting go of these items.

After discarding as many items as possible, organize the keepers into categories, such as gardening items, home maintenance supplies, auto equipment, patio furniture and outdoor cooking items, sporting goods, toys, workbench tools, machine tools, and household overflow (seasonal clothing, holiday decorations, card tables, cots). Group each category into a neat pile. Decide which are the most important piles, then make a prioritized list.

It seems like part of the house, but this shed was added onto the side of the garage. It provides welcome storage space on two levels, and creates a perfect platform for a children's play deck on top.

Activity Areas

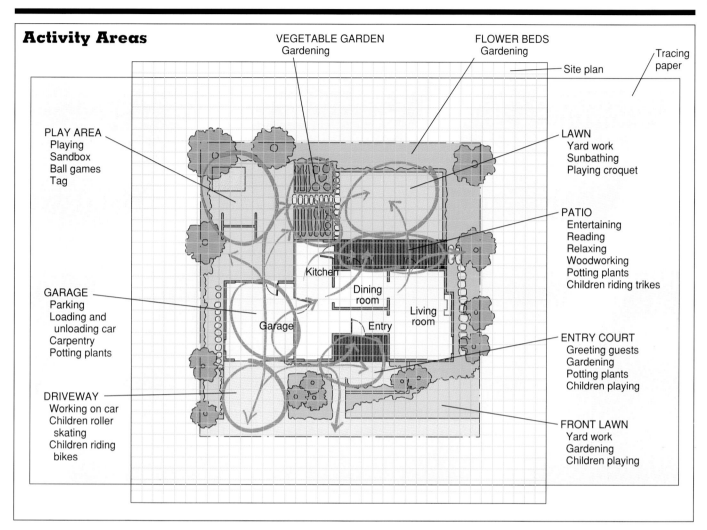

VEGETABLE GARDEN
Gardening

FLOWER BEDS
Gardening

Site plan

Tracing paper

PLAY AREA
Playing
Sandbox
Ball games
Tag

LAWN
Yard work
Sunbathing
Playing croquet

PATIO
Entertaining
Reading
Relaxing
Woodworking
Potting plants
Children riding trikes

Kitchen

Dining room

Living room

GARAGE
Parking
Loading and
 unloading car
Carpentry
Potting plants

Garage

Entry

ENTRY COURT
Greeting guests
Gardening
Potting plants
Children playing

DRIVEWAY
Working on car
Children roller
 skating
Children riding
 bikes

FRONT LAWN
Yard work
Gardening
Children playing

Step 2: Analyze the Site

Look at how your yard and home are used. Note unused spots. Follow the paths you take to find garden tools, sports equipment, children's toys, or extra chairs for outdoor entertaining. Notice how often people use gates or doorways.

To make it easier to analyze your yard, and to provide a tool that will be useful for other home improvement activities, make a site plan. It doesn't need to be to scale.

Next, lay a sheet of tracing paper over your plan and circle outdoor areas that your family uses, such as the area where you cook and eat, or spots where you frequently garden. Don't forget activities that occur in the garage or carport—parking, packing for trips, carpentry, auto maintenance, laundry.

Next, walk around the yard with your site plan. On a separate overlay, note all the objects that have been left outside, stacked in a corner, or strewn about the yard. This is how you will discover that some storage locations are fairly inconvenient.

Finally, list the problems you need to solve: "A place for the children's toys near the entry garden." "A place to pot plants, with space for potting soil, pots, and tools." Think about how you want a location to look, balancing practicality with aesthetics. If you prefer to have garden tools available near the patio, how can you keep it attractive for entertaining?

Step 3: Evaluate Your Storage Options

The hunt is on. Now that you've sorted your stuff and noted where storage is needed, you can look for potential storage spaces.

Utilize Existing Space

Using the space you already have is the most economical way to solve your storage problems. Look for ways to increase the efficiency and capacity of the spaces currently in use.

Garage or Carport

A garage is probably the most useful storage space because it's usually fairly large—capable of parking one or two cars plus storing additional items. It is weatherproof. It is often attached to the house and immediately accessible from it.

A garage is particularly suited to multiple-purpose storage, something most households need. It may be able to simultaneously accommodate gardening tools, a workbench, skis, camping equipment, and bicycles.

Even if your garage seems full, you may be able to add cabinets, shelves, or racks to store a wide assortment of objects.

A sheet of plywood laid across exposed roof ties or joists can accommodate rarely used and awkwardly shaped items, as long as they are relatively light. Objects such as a rubber raft or a kayak can be hung from the ties or joists.

The wood shingles and siding suit this shed to its natural setting.

Shed

You may have a shed that could be better utilized. Many sheds seem filled to capacity when actually it's only the floor that is cluttered. Shelves, racks, hangers, and other storage components on the walls and ceiling can make the space more efficient. You could shift the location of some items: If the shed is more convenient and accessible than the garage, move seldom-used items to the garage and utilize the freed-up shed space for things you use more often.

Exterior Walls

You can build a modified shed—a lean-to—virtually anywhere alongside the house if it does not block existing

windows and doors. Of course it should meet local code requirements. Using an exterior wall of the house—or garage or even a fence—in this way has a number of advantages: one wall is already in place, the shed ties to a strong existing structure, and there is direct access from the outside. In some cases, an exterior wall can be used to anchor shelves, racks, hose reels, cabinets, and other storage components without building any overhead structure.

Under a Deck

A deck that covers a sizable area of unused ground provides an excellent location for materials that can withstand rain and cold: lumber, pipe, roof gutters, certain types of bricks, and so on. You can simply slide these items under the deck. If you wish, add walls or skirting to conceal them.

There are several ways to elevate the stored items: lay pressure-treated 4×4s across concrete blocks, pour a concrete slab over part of the covered area, or suspend racks from the deck joists. (Such racks should be used only for very light loads, or enough racks should be used to distribute the load over several joists. Consult with an architect or a building contractor if you plan to store heavy loads.)

Consider making storage tubes out of large-diameter PVC pipes. They are readily available in 4- and 6-inch diameters; you can obtain pipes in larger diameters from agricultural supply outlets or other suppliers of irrigation and drainage materials. Stack the pipes under the deck and

slide materials into them. For moisture and critter protection, glue a cap onto one end of the pipe and slip an unglued cap onto the other end.

Add New Storage Space

If your house has no carport or garage, or the garage is full, it's time to think about adding a structure such as a shed. A separate shed will not only allow you to store three bicycles, a table saw, the lawnmower, and those tires you simply can't throw away, but it might free space in the garage for the workbench you've wanted for years. In addition, a shed may create all the additional storage you need, reducing your task to just one project. A well-designed shed, either purchased or built, can also be an attractive addition to the yard.

Step 4: Assign Storage Locations

It is time to decide what goes where. With a fresh sheet of tracing paper, start a working plan. Indicate the existing storage spaces, noting anything that cannot change or has top priority. Next, look at your prioritized list of stuff. Checking against your surveys of activity areas and problem spots, indicate on the plan the most convenient location for each item or category, using circles to show roughly how much space you need.

If you are planning a new shed, use your site plan and overlays to determine the most suitable location. Place the shed alongside but not over a traffic path, and near the area used for the activity associated with the stored items. Then list everything you plan to store in the shed; if you've not already done so, organize the list into groups of items that belong together. Determine how much space each group will require.

Step 5: Draw a Detailed Plan

Now decide how to use the spaces you have reserved for particular items. Think not only of the storage space but also of the space you will need when you stash and retrieve things.

To make a detailed plan for your existing spaces, measure the spaces carefully, then transfer the measurements to graph paper and draw a floor plan plus an elevation of each wall. Include features that might enhance your use of the space. Include door and window openings and electrical and water outlets—you'll want to avoid blocking any of them. Indicate the location of studs (whether exposed or not) so you can plan how to easily mount shelves, perforated board, and cabinets.

Experiment with ideas until you're satisfied, then make a clean copy of the final plan. It will be your guide as you proceed.

If you are building a new structure, follow the same process to delineate its dimensions and plan its interior. See page 10 for shed-planning guidelines.

Storing Hazardous Materials

Among the materials you are storing, you may have items that are hazardous from both safety and environmental standpoints. Follow the precautions on the label for storing all automotive and household cleaners, paints, garden chemicals, and similar materials. Keep them in their original containers, clearly labeled and tightly capped, in a locked, well-ventilated cabinet.

Shelves need to have lipped edges or rails to prevent containers from falling. If you live in earthquake country, you will need particularly secure storage. Rails on the shelves should be at half the height of the tallest container and sturdy enough that the heaviest container will not break through them. For easy access, rails this high may need to be hinged or otherwise movable.

Flammable substances, such as paints, gasoline, and bottled gases, should be stored in appropriate containers in a locked metal cabinet, separate from the house or garage if possible, and well away from heat sources.

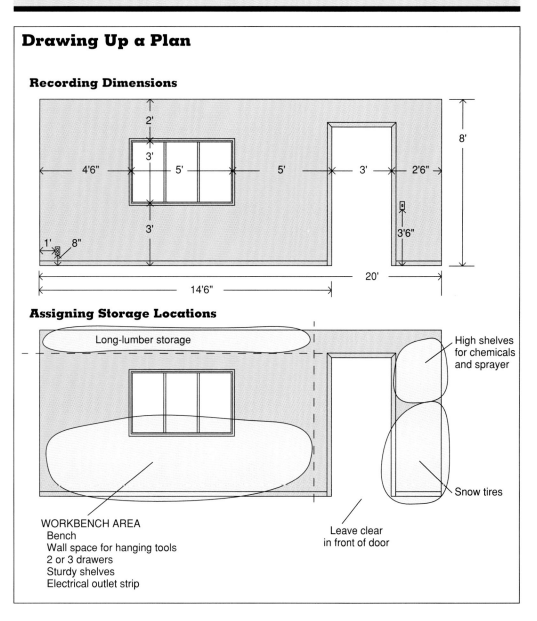

Drawing Up a Plan

Recording Dimensions

Assigning Storage Locations

Long-lumber storage

High shelves for chemicals and sprayer

Snow tires

Leave clear in front of door

WORKBENCH AREA
Bench
Wall space for hanging tools
2 or 3 drawers
Sturdy shelves
Electrical outlet strip

DESIGNING A STORAGE SHED

In many cases, you will have decided that a shed will solve your outdoor storage problems. Next comes deciding what kind of shed. The following considerations provide guidance in figuring out the ideal configuration.

To Buy or to Build?

At some point you'll need to decide whether to buy a shed or to build one from scratch. Although you won't need to make that decision now, keep it in mind as you design your ideal shed.

Buying a shed is certainly the fastest and simplest route. (For more information on purchasing a prefabricated shed, see page 16.) However, even the wide variety of structures available may not match your space or your particular requirements, including appearance. Building your own shed necessitates spending more time, effort, and probably money, but it gives you the flexibility to create just what you want. The shed plans in this book (see pages 19 to 79) will give you an idea of what is involved in building your own shed. The plans begin with a basic shed and progress to more complex designs. If a design appeals to you, study the designs presented earlier in this book, as well—they may include information that clarifies the more complex designs.

Considering Function

How you use the shed will influence the shape and size of the structure, the location of the door, the kind of materials you should use, where the shed should be located, and what fixtures you need to install in it. Consider the following issues.

• Who will use the shed? How tall are they? You may need to make high places accessible to a short adult or inaccessible to children. You may need to keep overhead space clear for the sake of a tall person's head.

• Will the shed be used for storage only, or do you intend to combine one or more activities with the storage function?

• What sizes and shapes are the items and equipment you will store?

• How much space will you need for active use (work or play), inactive use (storage), and transitional use (access)? Try to design a structure that is flexible enough so you can change its use as needed.

As you list the functional requirements of your shed, consider the implications each has for design. For instance, if you need to store pipes or lumber, the shed should be a little more than 20 feet long to accommodate full lengths. If you will be doing woodworking, the ceiling should be high enough (at least 10 feet) so you can manipulate long boards. If you will be spending time in the shed, consider a skylight or two for natural illumination. If you will be storing a lawn tractor or other large items in the shed, you'll want double doors for easy access. If you will be storing heavy materials in a shed with steps, include a ramp for wheelbarrows and carts. If you want a small shed but have some large items that you use frequently, you can extend the roof overhang to create a sheltered storage space outside the shed.

Considering Size

Several factors influence the size of a shed, including interior space requirements, foundation design, structural considerations, site limitations, budget, legal restrictions, and appearance. Some of these factors depend on your own preferences and needs, but others, such as local height limits or the maximum span of a 2×4, impose rigid restrictions. To juggle these factors, start with the functional needs you have already listed, and then adjust them, as needed, to accommodate other requirements.

Length and Width

How much floor area will you need? First, consider the largest and longest items that you intend to store, such as a sailboat mast, a canoe, or patio furniture, and plan the shed dimensions accordingly. Then, consider the items that must be stored on the floor, such as a lawn mower, wheelbarrow, garbage cans, tricycles, and so on, and estimate the amount of floor space required. Add the floor area required for any cabinets or floor-to-ceiling shelving you plan. Then add the floor space you need to stand and maneuver things.

Be thorough; draw sketches or make lists of every item or activity, and fit them together like a jigsaw puzzle to come up with the most efficient dimensions and shape for your shed. Remember that the more unbroken wall space your shed has (without windows or doors), the more capacity it will have for storing things in cabinets and on shelves, racks, and hooks. For that reason, consider interior partition walls.

You should also consider the floor area of your shed from an exterior perspective. How much ground will it cover? Many communities have lot-coverage limitations—the amount of your property that can be covered by the house, garage, decks, swimming pool, auxiliary buildings, and other structures. If you are already close to the limit, which may be about 40 percent of the total lot, you may have to plan the shed size very carefully to keep from exceeding the limit.

Appearance is another factor that might affect the floor dimensions, or footprint, of your shed. Think about the overall mass of the structure and the shape of the facade to be sure you will be happy with this shed in your yard.

Height

The shed's height should be determined by the interior space requirements, the foundation, and the roof pitch. At least part of the shed should be high enough that you can stand comfortably. This minimum height, usually

around 7 feet, when added to the foundation and the thickness of the floor and roof structures, means that the shed at its highest point could be well over 8 feet.

Local zoning laws or subdivision covenants, conditions, and restrictions (CC&Rs) may limit the height of the structure, especially if it is close to the property line. Many communities have an 8-foot limit for structures within the setback area; some have a 6-foot limit. Rules may vary according to whether the shed is considered a temporary or a permanent structure. Contact your local planning department or homeowners' association to find out what the restrictions are. In tight situations, you may be able to get around the height restrictions by changing the direction or shape of the roof slope.

Door Size

The size of a shed door calls for more thought than you might expect. Bulky items may require a door that is wider or higher than standard. You may find that you need extra elbow room to move items in and out by yourself; measure the large items again and think about how you will move them. Do you want your doors to open in or out? Perhaps sliding doors would be more efficient. Be sure to position the doors where they will provide clear access to your stored items, allowing you to remove and return things easily.

Shown here are the front and back of the same shed. The front (top) has a two-door "garage" for parking lawn and recreational vehicles, and a separate compartment with a workbench for woodworking tools and gardening supplies. The back of the shed (bottom) has equally large doors that provide access to a shallow storage space suitable for gardening tools and pet supplies.

Efficient Use of Materials

In planning the dimensions of a shed that you will build, consider the most efficient use of materials. Four is the magic number, the basic unit of many standard building dimensions. A standard sheet of plywood is 4 feet wide. The length of the standard sheet is twice the width—8 feet—which is the conventional height for walls. Divide 4 feet by three and you get 16 inches; divide it by two and you have 24 inches. These two dimensions are the standard spacings for wall studs, floor joists, ceiling joists, and rafters, ensuring that joints will align over framing members.

The illustration on page 25 shows a basic shed that measures 8 feet wide by 12 feet long, with walls 8 feet high.

These dimensions allow the maximum use of each sheet of plywood without requiring too many cuts or a lot of waste. The long walls are composed of two full sheets of plywood plus one half sheet. The width requires two full sheets. The only cuts are for windows. If the shed is greater than these dimensions by only a few inches, you will have to waste several sheets of plywood cutting and fitting.

Considering Appearance

As you plan your shed, consider it as an adornment for your yard. Should it be understated and avoid catching the eye, or should it be a major focal point characterized by charm, whimsy, or a distinct architectural style? Look through the designs and photographs in this book for styles that you like. Find out if your local codes, ordinances, community, or CC&Rs require or restrict particular materials and colors.

If you're not sure about style, the safest approach is to plan your shed to blend in with your home and yard. Match the materials of a fence or the house, including siding, roofing, windows, and trim. If you choose a different material—a metal shed, for instance—paint it the same color as the house. You can also camouflage the building with shrubs and plants. Build a frame and attach lattice on which to grow vines, or set the structure behind existing foliage.

Considering Climate and Site Factors

Every region has some harsh conditions that can damage or destroy structures and their contents. Design your shed to withstand the rigors of your location. There is no way to totally protect against hurricanes, tornadoes, torrential rains, and earthquakes, but sturdy design and construction can keep the structure safe in most circumstances.

As you design, remember that the most vulnerable areas are the roof and foundation. Be particularly aware of moisture, whether from flooding, seepage, or rain. It will rot wood, corrode metal, and spoil the contents of your shed with mildew. Be sure your design provides sufficient ventilation, so that natural dampness that results from humidity can evaporate.

Site and Foundation

Four types of foundations are suitable for sheds: skids, pier blocks, a concrete slab, and a solid perimeter. For more information on these options, see page 20.

Examine your land and determine the drainage pattern. If you have a choice of locations, place the structure away from low spots, in an area where water does not collect on the ground and where there will be no flow toward the foundation. If you have a single ideal location and it is subject to flooding, prepare the area by filling and grading or by digging drainage ditches to divert the water.

This shed is a major focal point of the backyard landscape. Its location, dimensions, and details all reflect the careful planning needed to successfully create such a garden highlight.

Know what type of soil you have. How dense is it? Ask the local building department, a geologist, or an engineering company. The kind of soil may determine the type of foundation your shed can have, or may dictate site preparation. If the soil is too soft, you may have to bring in gravel and compact the site. If you live in earthquake or high-wind territory, local codes may require a particular site preparation or type of foundation.

If you live in a region where the ground freezes, you must take this into account. Freezing causes moisture in the soil to expand, generally upward. Wherever the ground heaves, the building tends to skew on its foundation and pull apart, causing at the least cracked walls and sticking doors. To avoid these problems, either set the shed on a surface foundation, such as skids that rest on the earth, or dig footing holes down to dense, undisturbed soil, below the frost line.

If you are planning a slab foundation, remember that concrete absorbs water. A 6-mil sheet of plastic under the slab serves as an excellent vapor barrier to keep moisture from moving up through the slab into the building.

Roof

Some additional expense and attention to details now may prevent substantial losses from moisture damage later. The roof should have a slope steep enough that rain and snow will run off easily. A shingled roof needs a greater slope than one covered with

sheet material, to minimize the tendency of wind to blow water under the shingles, where it can rot the underlying wood and cause leaking.

A wide roof overhang carries rain runoff away from the building and protects the foundation from erosion or puddles of standing water. A wide overhang also prevents most rain from hitting the walls directly, which reduces weathering. Consider attaching roof gutters to collect runoff and drain it into a dry well or a ditch that slopes away from the building.

Although wood shakes and shingles are very attractive, they can catch fire from wind-blown sparks and flaming debris. Consider fiberglass and asphalt shingles or a strong mineral-surface roofing

that can withstand years of exposure to sun and storms.

If you live in snow country, the weather can be particularly harsh. It is essential that the roof be capable of bearing the weight of the accumulated snow. The crucial factor is the size and spacing of the rafters; commonly, snow-country rafters consist of 2×6 or 4×6 lumber set no more than 2 feet on center. A steep roof sheds snow more easily than a flat roof. Consult your local code, and don't compromise.

Ventilation

Air circulation is important. High heat and humidity not only make the structure uncomfortable, they can cause a breeding ground for mildew and rot. Proper ventilation will relieve both problems. At

a minimum, you should have vents in the gables. Consider screen or wire mesh vents between rafters in a number of places. Floor vents and (if you have a perimeter foundation) foundation vents can add to a continuous flow of fresh air.

Shear Strength and Anchoring

Wind and earthquakes exert lateral stress on walls and framing; earthquakes produce uplift—raising or thrusting upward from the ground. Properly braced walls can resist lateral forces, and good anchoring can minimize the effects of uplift.

Plywood or oriented strand board sheathing provides excellent bracing due to its shear strength. Steel straps and fasteners can provide

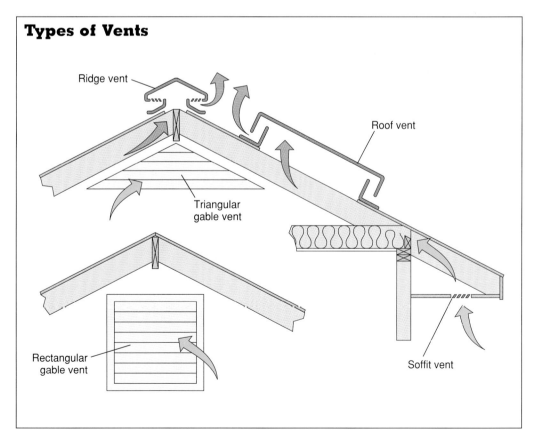

Types of Vents

Ridge vent

Roof vent

Triangular gable vent

Rectangular gable vent

Soffit vent

additional strength at joints. Consult local building codes, which usually take into account the speed and direction of prevailing winds and the likelihood of windstorms and earthquakes in your area.

Weatherproofing

Flashing, drip edge, caulk, sealants, and other weatherproofing materials can help make a structure watertight. Flashing around windows and doors prevents rain from blowing or seeping in through the casings, and it enhances the effects of insulation. If you have a shingle roof, add drip edge to prevent water from seeping under the shingles.

Fire Protection

People who live in dry areas, especially the West and the Southwest, need to be particularly conscious of fire. Buildings should be located away from flammable materials, and the surroundings should be kept clear of dry grasses, debris, and underbrush.

Choosing Materials

If you plan to build your storage shed, you have some choices in building materials. The following are available from lumberyards, hardware stores, and warehouse stores. You may also find used materials that fit your plan: windows, doors, glass, or salvage lumber and plywood. If you plan to use found materials, be certain they conform to current building standards and that you can easily incorporate them into your plan.

Wood

The most suitable and economical material for small structures is wood. It possesses strength and durability. It is easy to use in construction and desirable in appearance. The softwoods—fir, pine, hemlock, spruce, larch, cedar, cypress, and redwood—are particularly useful. Although cedar and redwood are generally resistant to rot and insects, only the heartwood of these species has that characteristic, and heartwood is considerably more expensive than other species.

Pressure-Treated Lumber

Chemically treated to resist decay and insects, pressure-treated lumber is particularly effective wherever wood comes into direct contact with the ground or a concrete foundation. Check the rating. Some pressure-treated wood is rated for direct burial uses (such as posts); some is suitable only for above-grade uses (sill plates or soleplates of walls, and framing members). Pressure-treated wood usually has a characteristic green or brown tint, sometimes with incision marks. If the wood will be exposed, it should be painted or stained. Paint and stain do not degrade its durability.

Structural Lumber

Douglas fir and yellow pine are the most common structural woods, but many others will do just as well; ask your local lumberyard for recommendations. Structural lumber is usually available either surfaced or unsurfaced. Unsurfaced wood comes in full dimensions; surfaced wood is smaller. An unsurfaced 2×4 is a full 2 inches thick and 4 inches wide; a surfaced 2×4 is 1½ inches by 3½ inches.

All structural lumber has a stamp that indicates its grade, mill of origin, wood species, grading agency, and whether it is green (S-grn) or seasoned (S-dry). Green lumber is much less expensive and is fine for shed construction. For posts, joists, rafters, and other important load-bearing members, choose a "No. 2 or Better" grade of lumber. Use lower grades of lumber—"Construction," "Standard," and "Utility" grades—for light loads,

The builder of this shed wanted some of its materials to be resistant to decay. The 2×4 soleplate, for instance, is pressure-treated lumber because it is in direct contact with the foundation. The plywood siding is stained and treated for exterior exposure, and the nails are galvanized.

blocking, nonbearing partition walls, and other less structural purposes. "Stud"-grade lumber is for vertical members and is normally precut to standard stud lengths. For the greatest strength, use "No. 1" lumber or, where appearance is important, "Select Structural."

Finish Lumber

Where appearance matters, a higher-quality softwood such as redwood, fir, cedar, or pine with few, if any, knots is particularly appropriate. Finish lumber is usually used for window and door casings, moldings, trim, and interior finish. Finish lumber is usually no thicker than 2 inches.

Plywood

This versatile material consists of wood veneers laminated in alternating layers at 90 degrees to one another. Great strength and stability make plywood ideal for floors and for roof and wall sheathing. Since it comes in 4×8 panels, it covers a large surface quickly, which facilitates rapid construction.

Structural plywood is graded on each side from A to D; A is best, with virtually no knots or defects. With a piece of AC, the A surface is best and should face outward. CDX is particularly good for floors, shear walls, and roofing. The X indicates exterior, meaning it is made with moistureproof glue. Panels marked "interior-exterior glue" can withstand wetness without delaminating.

Various thicknesses are suitable for different purposes. Panels of ⅜-inch and ½-inch plywood with exterior glue are useful for siding. Some have patterns or grooves sawed into the face. The most useful sizes for roofing are ½-inch and ⅝-inch plywood; the thicker grade should be used in areas where heavy snow loads are likely. Floors need the heaviest grades: ⅝ inch to 1⅛ inches depending upon the uses, expected loads, and spacing of floor joists.

Similar to plywood and virtually equal in strength and durability is oriented strand board (also known as OSB). It consists of large wood chips compressed with exterior glue into alternating cross-patterned layers. OSB comes in 4×8 sheets the same thicknesses as plywood, from ½ inch to 1⅛ inches. Its applications are identical to those of CDX plywood: for flooring, shear walls, siding, and roofing. In some areas, oriented strand board is less expensive than plywood.

Concrete

A concrete perimeter foundation or slab is a very stable base for most locations and buildings. Concrete is relatively inexpensive, fairly easy to work with, and definitely durable. You can pour it yourself or order a delivery of premixed concrete.

Figure what you need by the cubic yard (27 cubic feet). A five-sack mix is adequate for most backyard structures. (Sack refers to the number of sacks of Portland cement per cubic yard of concrete.) If you are planning a pier-and-post foundation, it is probably more economical to mix concrete for the footings yourself with a small cement mixer, or manually in a trough or a wheelbarrow. Use precast concrete piers with metal brackets or pressure-treated blocks embedded in them.

Roofing Material

The choice of roofing materials depends upon the shape and slope of your roof. Flatter roofs will require continuous materials with the fewest possible seams. Steeper slopes afford the opportunity for more interesting materials.

Whatever your finish roofing material, cover the underlying plywood or board sheathing with the proper underlayment. Over that, you can lay 90-pound mineral surface roll roofing or the shingles of your choice (composition, wood, slate, cement, terra-cotta). Estimate and order roofing material in "squares"; each square is enough material to cover 100 square feet.

Hardware and Other Materials

You will need an array of hardware: fasteners, nails, screws, anchor bolts, and connectors (such as joist hangers, post caps, T-straps, and corner braces). Flashing or drip edge is essential wherever different materials and/or parts of the structure meet—along roof ridges and valleys, vents, doors, windows, wall/roof junctions, and roof edges. Don't forget hinges, doorknobs, door slides (if you plan to have sliding doors), and locks. All hardware should have corrosion-resistant coatings. Prehung doors (manufactured with frames attached) are easy to install. You may be able to locate some that are perfect for your purpose. Add caulk, glue, primer, weatherstripping, and paint or stain to your list.

PREFAB SHEDS

Prefabricated sheds are quick to erect and locally available in a fairly wide variety. Prices vary. Quality kits generally come with all the instructions and materials you need except a solid foundation.

Planning for a Prefab

Prefabricated sheds are available at retail outlets and also through certain mail-order catalogs. Some companies provide installation.

Before ordering a prefabricated shed, examine an assembled one and read a set of assembly instructions (manufacturers usually provide these upon request). Check the construction. Be sure that the materials are sturdy and the design is compatible with local codes. Will the structure withstand local climatic conditions and the uses that you intend? How easy is it to assemble? Is the kit complete?

Plan to locate a metal shed away from trees that drop nuts, cones—even leaves and sticks. Falling debris can easily dent, weaken, or even puncture the roof. Decide what you want to do about a foundation. Some manufacturers sell separately a foundation of pressure-treated wood that can sit on the ground, on gravel, or on a slab. Others include directions for constructing foundations.

When you receive the kit, be certain it has all the parts, a complete parts list, and detailed instructions for assembly. Prepare the site, being sure it is level.

Metal Sheds

Storage sheds made of metal are generally utilitarian structures; distinguished design is not one of their strong points. Low cost is their greatest advantage. Their disadvantage is that the thin sheet metal dents easily. As long as the metal is intact, the structure will perform well. Sheds that conform to the standards of the American Society for Testing and Materials have met minimum requirements for basic material strength.

Erecting a Metal Shed

Most metal sheds are "ready to go," and there is little you can do to alter their appearance, so be certain you have the style you want.

Metal sheds are easy to put together, but because the metal is so easily damaged, do not try to erect one yourself. Avoid putting it together on a windy day; light sheet metal can sail dangerously in the wind. Wear sturdy work gloves—the metal edges and corners are very sharp.

Assembly is normally fairly simple. You need a screwdriver, pliers, a stepladder, an awl for aligning holes, work gloves, and tools for preparing the foundation and anchoring the structure.

Metal Shed With Gable Roof
Interior: Connecting Roof to Walls

Metal Prefab Shed With Gambrel Roof

Because sheet metal is vulnerable to strong winds, anchoring is important. Bolt the structure to a foundation, or secure it with special anchors that you can screw like an auger through the base directly into the ground, or with cables that you string over the shed's beams and fasten to the ground with anchors.

You might want to use 2×2 lumber inside the shed along the joints at the floor, roof, and corners to provide more structural integrity (see right). Consider bolting the shed onto pressure-treated 2×4s to keep it from direct contact with concrete, gravel, or dirt.

Check that the door opens smoothly and easily. Any difficulty now will probably worsen in the future, weakening that part of the building.

Wood Sheds

Retail outlets sell specially manufactured lines of wood buildings that can serve a number of purposes. Ranging from small playhouses to large sheds, they come in a wide variety of styles. You can order these in kit form or already assembled. Before you order, do some research. See what is on the market in your locale before you make a decision.

Prefab wood sheds are often sturdier and heavier than metal sheds. It is a good idea to build a foundation to anchor the structure and keep it off the ground. See page 20 for foundation options.

Some wood kits are pre-painted or primed, but most require paint or stain as protection against the elements.

Reinforcing a Metal Shed

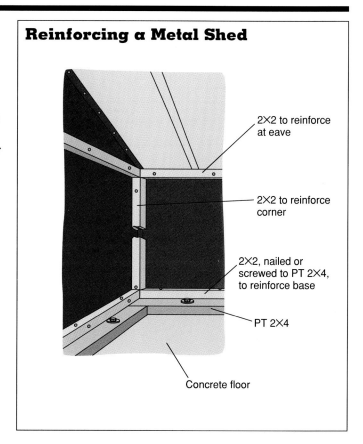

2×2 to reinforce at eave

2×2 to reinforce corner

2×2, nailed or screwed to PT 2×4, to reinforce base

PT 2×4

Concrete floor

Wood Prefab Shed With Gable Roof

Wood Shed With Gambrel Roof

BASIC STORAGE SHEDS

This chapter presents four relatively simple—yet substantial—sheds that can be built by a person with basic carpentry skills. Each design reflects a particular style and is intended for a specific function. Each has a complete materials list and illustrated building instructions.

The Basic Gable-Roofed Shed, which appears first, incorporates most of the standard construction techniques used in building a light-framed structure. If you intend to build one of the other designs in this chapter or the following chapter, refer to the basic shed for more complete information on building techniques.

All of the shed designs contain fairly precise dimensions and specifications. You can adapt them to your own needs and preferences, but if you change a design, remember to alter the materials list as well. Although the designs in this book call for specific foundations, you can choose any of the foundations discussed at the beginning of this chapter, depending upon the size of the structure.

Any of the basic shed designs in this chapter can be enhanced by a few simple details. Notice how the scalloped trim, crisp color scheme, and hanging plant give this diminutive shed—less than 7 feet wide—a strong personality.

FOUNDATION OPTIONS

When building a shed, you have a choice of four types of foundations: skids, pier blocks (or buried posts), a concrete slab, and a solid perimeter. The most appropriate type for your shed depends upon your budget, the size of the shed, structural requirements, site restrictions, and your preferences.

Skids

Little more than 2 logs laid on the ground, skids are the simplest foundation. Appropriate mainly for small sheds, skids imply a temporary structure that can be moved from place to place, although skids work fine for small buildings intended to stay put. There are 3 keys to a successful skid foundation: a stable base, rot-resistant lumber, and secure connections to the shed.

For the base, install 6 to 8 inches of crushed rock, road base, or coarse gravel over

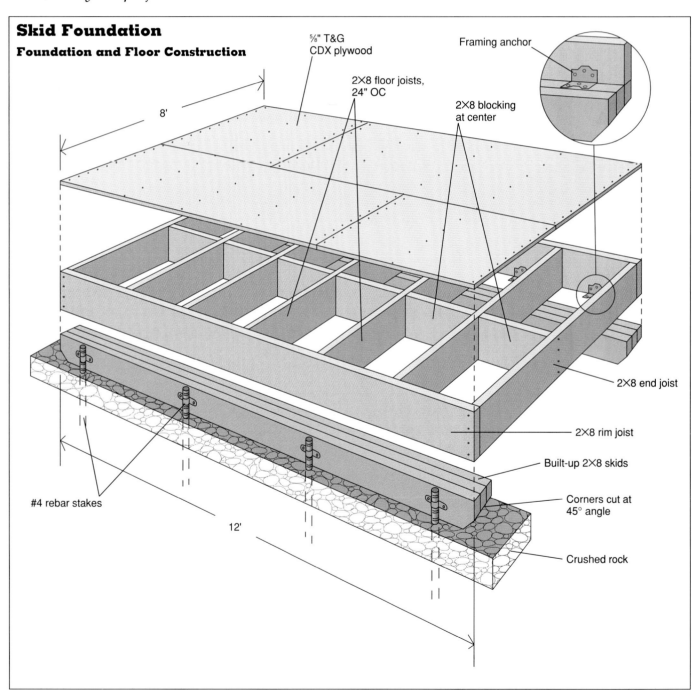

Skid Foundation

Foundation and Floor Construction

⅝" T&G CDX plywood

2×8 floor joists, 24" OC

2×8 blocking at center

Framing anchor

8'

2×8 end joist

2×8 rim joist

Built-up 2×8 skids

Corners cut at 45° angle

Crushed rock

#4 rebar stakes

12'

well-drained soil. This base ensures rapid drainage, discourages the growth of weeds and rot-causing organisms, minimizes frost heaves, and allows the shed to adjust to ground settling. In dry locations you can limit the gravel to 2 strips under the skids, each strip 12 inches wide by 4 inches deep.

For the skids, use pressure-treated lumber, either solid timbers, or beams built up from 2-by lumber. They should be at least 4½ inches wide on the bottom. Angle the bottoms of the ends; should you want to move the shed, this will make it easier to pull it along the ground.

To fabricate a built-up beam, cut three 2×8s to the length of the shed and nail them together with 16-penny (16d) hot-dipped galvanized (HDG) common nails, two at each end and one every 16 inches alternately at the top and bottom edge of the beam.

Lay the skids on edge so that the outside faces will be flush with the outside edges of the shed floor. Check to see that the skids are parallel and square by measuring the diagonals; make adjustments as necessary. To stabilize the skids, drive rebar or wood stakes into the ground along the sides. Level the skids by tamping them into the gravel at high spots with a sledge-hammer or by filling in gravel beneath low spots.

When you frame the floor, toenail the joists into the skids with 8d HDG common nails. Then reinforce the connections with L-shaped steel framing anchors nailed into the skids and rim joists with 1¼-inch HDG fastener nails. Space connectors every 24 to 32 inches.

Piers

Precast pier blocks can provide a stable foundation for a shed as long as you prepare the site properly. If you need to dig down more than a few inches to level the site, check with local authorities on the location of underground pipes and gas and electric lines. Also look out for shallow irrigation pipes and TV cables.

When you are sure that the shed site is where you want it in relation to the house, fences, property lines, and local setback requirements, proceed by establishing the corners and boundaries of the shed. Ensure that the layout is square by measuring the diagonals between opposite corners, then stake the corners. Erect batter boards (see page 22) and stretch nylon string along the building dimensions.

Lay out the pier blocks, 4 feet on center, using as a guide the batter boards and the nylon string lines that represent the outside edge of each wall. Make certain that the ground is level wherever you place the pier blocks. Mark the location of each block, then move each one aside to dig the footing hole (at least 6 inches deep and 18 inches square). Fill each hole with concrete, then set the pier blocks into the concrete 1 inch deep. Before the concrete sets, make sure that each block is level and aligned with the others; this is essential for a level floor.

Depending upon height restrictions and any limitations imposed by the hazards of earthquakes and wind, the girders can be either attached directly to the pier blocks or elevated on 4×4 posts. If the pier blocks you are using have pressure-treated wood blocks embedded in them, toenail the girder to each block with 4 nails. If the pier blocks have metal brackets embedded in them, bolt the girder to each bracket. If you want to elevate the shed on 4×4 posts, place the girders on the posts and attach them with steel connectors. Check local building codes; some require 12- to 18-inch clearance below the floor joists. Wood girders should be pressure-treated and be at least 8 inches above grade.

An alternative to concrete pier blocks, especially where the frost line is deep, is to bury pressure-treated 6×6 posts in the ground where you would otherwise place pier blocks. With a posthole digger or an auger, dig holes to a depth below the frost line. Lay a bed of crushed rock, place the posts, and backfill around the posts with crushed rock. Cut off the posts so that the tops are all level and at least 8 inches above the ground. Then install girders over them, attached with steel connectors.

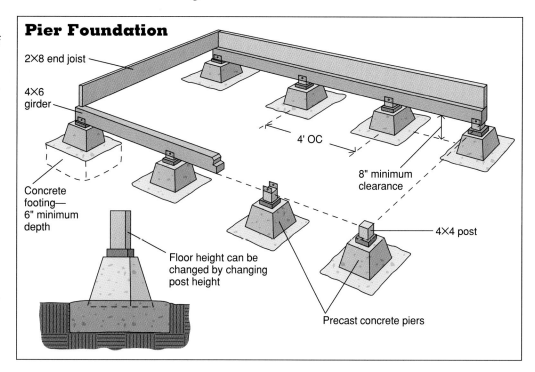

Pier Foundation

2×8 end joist

4×6 girder

Concrete footing— 6" minimum depth

Floor height can be changed by changing post height

4' OC

8" minimum clearance

4×4 post

Precast concrete piers

Concrete Slab

A 4-inch-thick concrete slab foundation has several advantages. It is rigid and durable.

It keeps the shed low, possibly eliminating the need for a ramp or steps. It combines foundation and floor construction into one operation.

Prepare the ground by removing all sod and organic debris and leveling high spots with a hoe and shovel. Tamp the soil to compact it. Level

and tamp it once more. Stake 2×8 form boards around the outside edge, making sure the corners are square (measure the diagonals) and the boards

Building Batter Boards

Batter boards allow you to lay out a foundation with string lines that can be adjusted, leveled, and moved easily. The batter boards, which are horizontal boards nailed to 2 stakes, should be set back from the foundation corners far enough to be out of the way of construction activity—usually 3 to 6 feet.

To build them, first drive a pair of 2×4 stakes into the ground, 3 feet apart, for each horizontal board. Then, using a water level, builder's level, or line level, mark each stake at a point that is level with the marks on all the other stakes. If

necessary, measure up from these marks a uniform distance to make the horizontal boards high enough to clear any foundation forms.

Then, nail a 1×4 across each pair of stakes, aligning the top of the board with the 2 marks. When all the horizontal boards are in place, brace any loose stakes with diagonal bracing. Stretch nylon mason's twine between opposite pairs of boards, tying it temporarily to nails in the tops of the boards. The 4 string lines form a rectangle whose dimensions should be the same as the

outside dimensions specified for the foundation walls. Adjust the nails and lines, as necessary, until all 4 dimensions are accurate.

Check to see if the corners are square by measuring the diagonals between corners. They should be equal. If not, adjust the nails and lines and recheck all dimensions until all sides are the correct length and the 4 corners are square.

You can untie the strings from the nails at any time to get them out of the way, then reattach them whenever necessary to guide construction.

Building Batter Boards

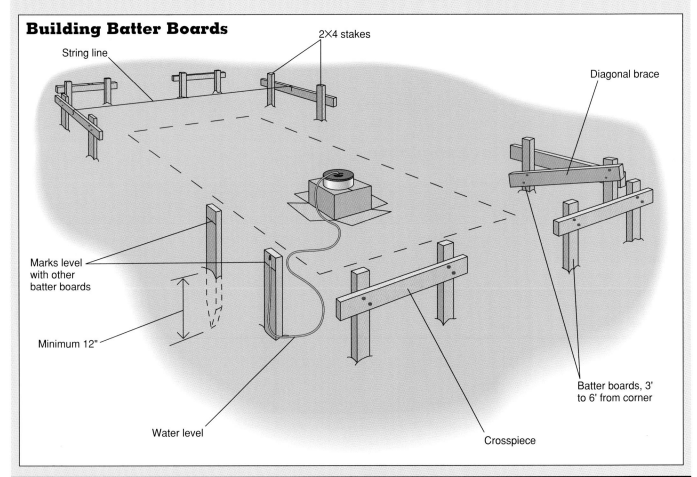

String line · 2×4 stakes · Diagonal brace · Marks level with other batter boards · Minimum 12" · Water level · Crosspiece · Batter boards, 3' to 6' from corner

Concrete Slab Foundation

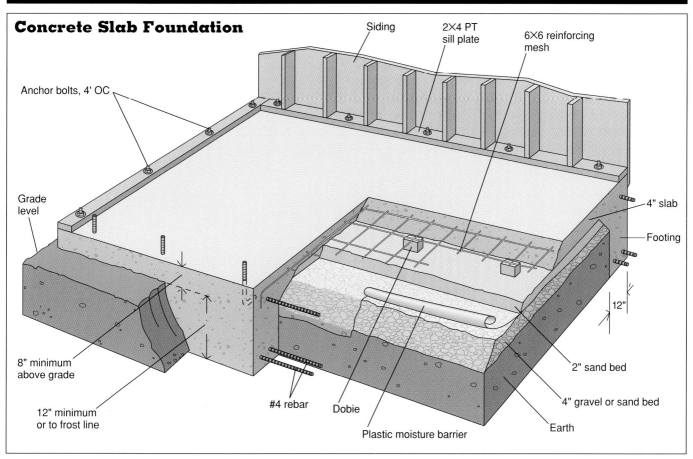

- Siding
- 2×4 PT sill plate
- 6×6 reinforcing mesh
- Anchor bolts, 4' OC
- Grade level
- 4" slab
- Footing
- 8" minimum above grade
- 12"
- 12" minimum or to frost line
- #4 rebar
- Dobie
- 2" sand bed
- 4" gravel or sand bed
- Earth
- Plastic moisture barrier

Concrete Slab Foundation Detail

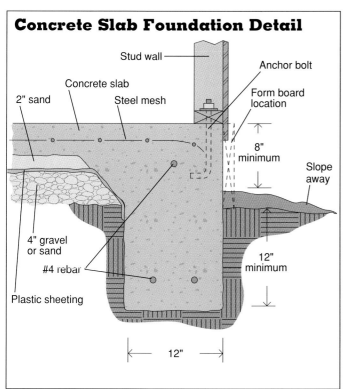

- Stud wall
- Anchor bolt
- Concrete slab
- Steel mesh
- Form board location
- 2" sand
- 8" minimum
- Slope away
- 4" gravel or sand
- 12" minimum
- #4 rebar
- Plastic sheeting
- 12"

are level, with the top edges 8 inches above grade.

Since the edges of the slab will serve as footings for the shed walls, reinforce the perimeter by digging a trench 12 inches wide and 12 inches deep (or to frost line, if it's feasible to dig so deep) inside the forms (see above and left). Within the perimeter created by the inside edge of the trench, lay 4 inches of gravel or sand, then cover it with 6-mil plastic sheeting for a moisture barrier. Cover this with 2 inches of sand.

Finally, place 2-inch concrete blocks, called dobies, 3 feet apart on the sand. Rest steel reinforcing mesh on the dobies, extending it over the trench; it will be centered horizontally in the 4-inch concrete.

In the trench, place lengths of No. 4 rebar on 3-inch dobies. Suspend a second course of rebar from the mesh, parallel to the first course and about an inch below the mesh. Now you're ready to pour.

For any amount of concrete over 1 yard, plan to order a ready-mix. (Concrete is sold by the cubic yard, which is 27 cubic feet. An 8-foot by 12-foot slab, with 12-inch-deep footings, requires approximately 2.8 yards of concrete.) If the concrete truck cannot back directly to the site, arrange for a pump truck as well; have both companies coordinate the delivery. Order some extra concrete just in case, and have several helpers on hand.

Pour the concrete, and consolidate it with a concrete

vibrator or by moving a stick up and down into the mix, especially in the footings. Once the concrete fills the forms, screed it off by dragging a 10-foot 2×4 in a sawing motion across the tops of the form boards. Smooth the surface with a wood float.

Before the concrete starts to set up, place anchor bolts into the concrete, 4 feet on center around the perimeter. When the concrete has set, texture the surface with a steel trowel or broom, depending upon the look you want.

Perimeter Foundation

Very stable, a perimeter foundation is ideal for supporting a raised floor. It consists of a continuous underground footing of poured concrete, supporting a wall of concrete blocks or poured concrete that extends 8 inches above the ground. The footing is 12 inches wide and 8 inches thick; its lowest edge is a minimum of 12 inches below grade or to the frost line (see detail at right). This type of foundation is not suitable for extremely cold climates, where digging very deep trenches to the frost line is not worth the effort.

Whether the foundation wall will be concrete blocks or poured concrete, first level the site and establish the corners with batter boards and string (see page 22). Then, using the string lines as a guide, dig 12-inch-wide footing trenches. The outside edges of the trenches should be 2 inches outside the string lines if the wall will be 8-inch-wide concrete blocks; allow

3 inches if it will be a 6-inch-wide poured-concrete wall. Keep the bottoms of the trenches level, and square the corners. Do not overdig or the wall will require too much concrete.

For concrete-block walls, place rebar along the bottom of the trench on 3-inch dobies; bend it around the corners. Install vertical rebars every 3 to 4 feet so that they align with the cells of the blocks. (To make vertical rebars, bend 3 inches of a 24-inch length of No. 4 rebar at a 90-degree angle.) Wire the vertical rebars to the horizontal ones, extending upward.

As with a slab, order a ready-mix concrete delivery and, if necessary, a pumper truck. Distribute 8 inches of concrete in the bottom of the trench, then level it with a wood float. If code requires, place a beveled 2×4 along the top of the footing to create a keyway, a slot that the mortar will fill to stabilize the wall.

After the concrete sets, lay 3 courses of 8-inch by 8-inch by 16-inch concrete blocks. Leave one block out of each wall so that you can install masonry-sized foundation vents. Fill the hollows of the blocks with concrete. Insert ½-inch by 10-inch anchor bolts into the poured concrete every 4 feet around the perimeter and within 6 inches of each end of each wall segment; make sure that at least 3 inches of the bolt extends above the concrete. After 24 hours, cut the pressure-treated 2×6 sill plates to length, drill holes in them to accommodate the anchor bolts, and bolt the sill plates to the foundation.

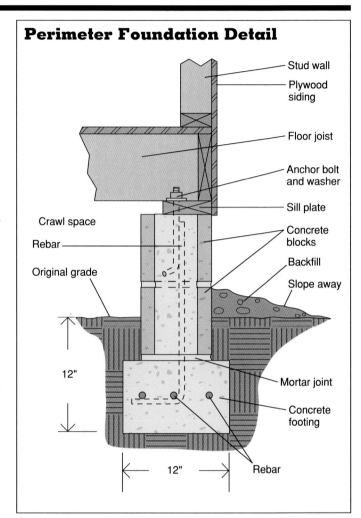

Perimeter Foundation Detail

Stud wall
Plywood siding
Floor joist
Anchor bolt and washer
Sill plate
Crawl space
Rebar
Original grade
Concrete blocks
Backfill
Slope away
12"
Mortar joint
Concrete footing
12"
Rebar

For a poured-concrete wall, pound steel foundation stakes 3 feet apart in a row in the bottom of the trench, with the inside edge of the stakes 1½ inches outside the string lines. Pound a second row of stakes into the trench 9 inches inside the first row.

Build forms by nailing 2-by lumber to the inside edges of both rows of stakes. Align the top edges of the forms with the string lines so that they are at the finished height of the foundation wall (usually 8 inches above grade). The bottoms of the forms will be suspended about 12 inches above the bottom of the trench.

Place 2 rebars along the bottom of the trench, on 3-inch dobies, and one centered just below the top of the forms, held in place by tie wire. Use foundation ties (available at home centers and lumberyards; insert between the form boards), braces, and extra stakes to stabilize the forms.

Pour in the concrete, vibrate it, and screed it level with the tops of the form boards. Insert anchor bolts as for a concrete-block wall. At day's end, remove the stakes. After 24 hours you can bolt on the sill plates and frame the floor, but leave the forms, at least on the outside, for 5 days.

BASIC GABLE-ROOFED SHED

This 8×12 shed provides simple, ample, versatile storage space. An experienced builder with one helper could put this up in 1½ days. A novice or do-it-yourselfer should count on spending roughly 6 days to erect this type of shed. The building techniques presented here are applicable to any structure.

Building the Floor

The foundation for this shed is post and pier, with 4×6 girders, but framing is the same as for a skid or perimeter foundation. For a slab foundation, skip the floor framing and proceed with the walls; frame walls with pressure-treated lumber for the sill plates and nail them to the studs with rust-resistant HDG nails, not uncoated or vinyl-coated nails.

Build a standard subfloor consisting of 2×8 joists and ⅝-inch CDX plywood. First, toenail the 2 rim joists to the girders (or skids or sill plates). Then place the field joists, 16 inches on center, between the rim joists, and nail each end with three 16d HDG common nails. Secure the rim joists to the girders with framing anchors, using 1¼-inch HDG hanger nails. Install 2×8 blocking between the joists down the center.

Install the plywood across the joists, with joints centered over the joists or the blocking. Stagger the end joints. Nail with 8d common nails, 6 inches on center at the edges and 12 inches on center in the field. Leave 1/16-inch gaps on the ends and ⅛-inch gaps on the sides of the plywood for expansion.

Framing the Walls

Frame the long walls to run the full 12-foot length of the structure. Frame the gable walls to fit between the long walls. After you cut the top and soleplates, lay out the studs, 16 inches on center, the door and window king studs and trimmer studs, and the rough framing for the windows and doors. Place additional studs with blocking at the ends of the long walls. When the layout is complete, nail the studs and plates together with 16d HDG common nails.

Raise the walls into place and nail the sill plates to the joists with 16d nails, 16 inches on center. Temporarily brace each wall to the floor with 1-by or 2-by boards.

Connect the walls to each other at the corners with 16d nails, and lap the cap plates for the gable walls over the long walls. Nail the cap plates to the top plates with 16d nails staggered every 24 inches. Add temporary diagonal braces inside each wall; these will remain in place until you have framed the roof and installed the siding. Once the walls are in place, you can saw out the sill plate in the door opening and add building paper to the outside walls.

Adding a Ramp

For the ramp, build a frame out of pressure-treated 2×6s and cover it with 2×6 decking (see the ramp detail on page 28). The length and cutting angles of the stringers will vary with the height of the shed floor, the slope of the ground, and the desired steepness of the ramp.

Basic Gable-Roofed Shed

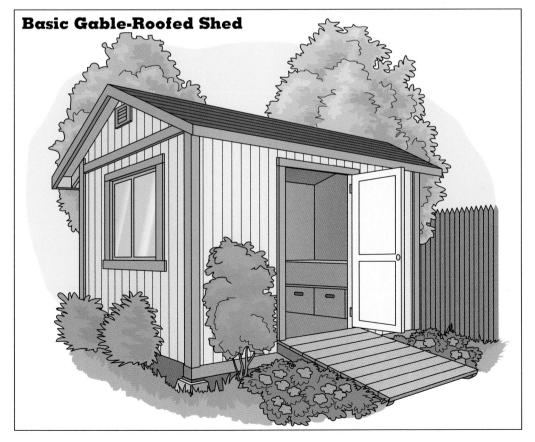

The preferred slope for a residential ramp is 1:8 (1 inch of rise for every 8 inches of horizontal run); if the ramp is too long you could make it slightly steeper or rest the bottom on a mound of fill 5 to 6 feet from the shed. Experiment with different angles by laying a plank up to the doorway and pushing a wheelbarrow up it. When you find a satisfactory slope and length, turn the plank on edge so it won't sag and tack it against the edge of the doorway so it won't move.

To mark and cut the 2×6 stringers for the ramp, use a bevel gauge to measure the angle at which the plank intersects the shed wall, then transfer that angle to one end of the stringer stock. Measure along the bottom edge of the plank from the doorway to the ground and transfer that distance to the top edge of the stringer. Using the bevel gauge again, mark the cutting line for the bottom of the stringer where it rests on the ground. Cut out the stringer

Anatomy of Basic Gable-Roofed Shed

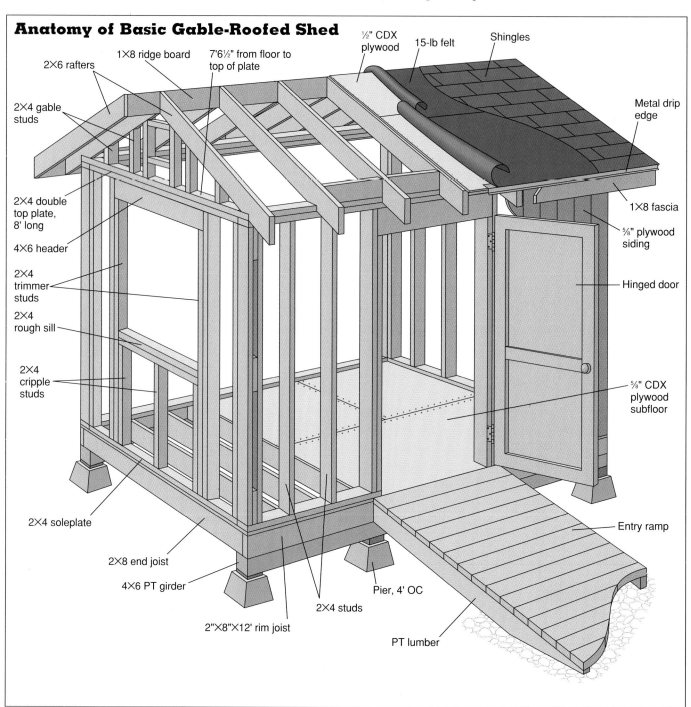

- 2×6 rafters
- 1×8 ridge board
- 7'6½" from floor to top of plate
- ½" CDX plywood
- 15-lb felt
- Shingles
- 2×4 gable studs
- Metal drip edge
- 1×8 fascia
- ⅝" plywood siding
- 2×4 double top plate, 8' long
- 4×6 header
- 2×4 trimmer studs
- 2×4 rough sill
- 2×4 cripple studs
- Hinged door
- ⅝" CDX plywood subfloor
- 2×4 soleplate
- 2×8 end joist
- 4×6 PT girder
- Pier, 4' OC
- 2×4 studs
- 2"×8"×12' rim joist
- PT lumber
- Entry ramp

and use it as a pattern for the second stringer.

Complete the ramp by cutting a 40-inch 2×6 ledger and attaching the top ends of the stringer to it with joist hangers or other connectors. Cut a 37-inch 2×6 crosspiece and nail it between the stringers near the bottom end. Lift the ramp frame into place and bolt the ledger into the floor framing with ½-inch by 3½-inch lag screws. Support the lower ends of the stringers on concrete piers, a bed of

Basic Gable-Roofed Shed Materials List

Description	Material/Size	Dimension	Qty
Foundation			
Piers	Precast	12" × 12"	8
Concrete	Premixed	80 lb	14 bags
Floor & wall framing			
Girders	4×6 PT	12'	2
Joists	2×8 PT	8'	10
	2×8 PT	12'	2
Blocking	2×8 PT	12'	1
Subfloor	⅝" CDX ply.	4×8	3
Soleplates	2×4	8'	2
	2×4	12'	2
Studs & misc	2×4	8'	48
Top & cap plates	2×4	12'	4
	2×4	8'	4
Headers	4×6	6'	2
Roof			
Rafters	2×6	6'	18
Blocking	2×4	12'	2
Collar ties	2×4	6'	5
Ridge board	1×8	14'	1
Sheathing	½" CDX ply.	4×8	6
Fascia	1×8	14'	2
	1×4	12'	4
Underlayment	15-lb felt	196 s.f.	1 roll
Drip edge	Galvanized	10'	7
Shingles	Composition		162 s.f.
Exterior finish			
Windows	Aluminum sliding	3'0" × 3'0"	2
Siding	⅝" ACX ply.	4×8	11
Field-built doors	2×4	8'	3
	ACX ply. (cut from above)	3'0" × 6'8"	1
Ramp	2×6 PT	12'	5
Paint/stain			2 gal.
Trim	1×4	12'	2
	1×4	9'	4
	1×3	8'	4

End Wall Construction

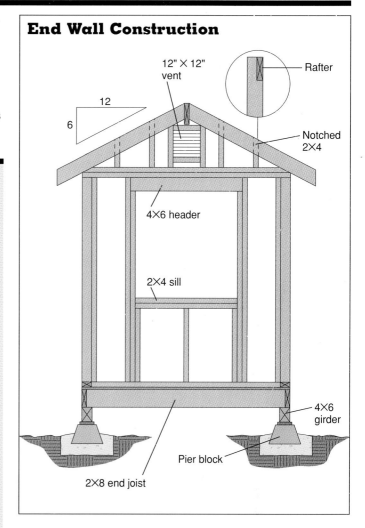

Materials List (continued)

Description	Material/Size	Dimension	Qty
Hardware & misc			
Steel stakes	#4, ½" dia	24"	8
Gable vents	Galvanized	12" × 12" (net)	2
Framing anchors	Simpson A34 or equiv		8
Nails & screws	As needed		
Hasp			1
Hook & eye			1
Butt hinges	3" steel		1 pair
Z flashing	Galvanized	8'	2
Attic vents	Louvered	18" × 24"	2
Building paper			360 s.f.
Roll flashing	4" aluminum		60 l.f.
Sealant			2 tubes
Construction adhesive for the door			2 tubes

Ramp Detail

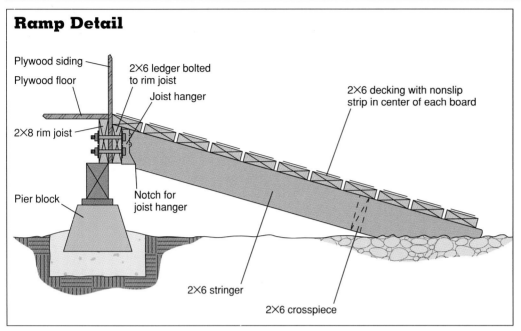

Plywood siding

Plywood floor

2×6 ledger bolted to rim joist

Joist hanger

2×8 rim joist

2×6 decking with nonslip strip in center of each board

Pier block

Notch for joist hanger

2×6 stringer

2×6 crosspiece

crushed rock, or a concrete landing. Then lay 2×6 decking across the stringers and nail each board with two 16d HDG nails in each stringer. Attach nonskid strips.

Building the Roof

The roof slope for this shed is 6 in 12. Follow the rafter diagram below and cut two 2×6 rafters. To do this, place a framing square near one end of the rafter stock so that the shorter leg of the square intersects the edge of the board at the 6-inch mark and the longer leg intersects the edge of the

Roof Framing and Assembly

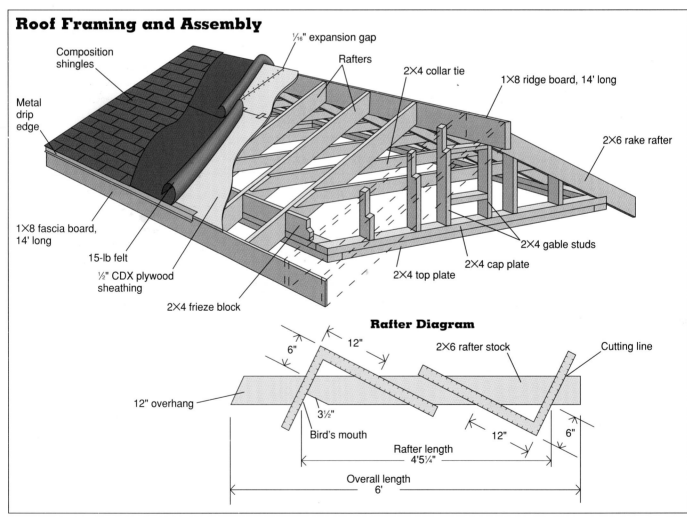

Composition shingles

Metal drip edge

1/16" expansion gap

Rafters

2×4 collar tie

1×8 ridge board, 14' long

2×6 rake rafter

1×8 fascia board, 14' long

15-lb felt

1/2" CDX plywood sheathing

2×4 frieze block

2×4 top plate

2×4 cap plate

2×4 gable studs

Rafter Diagram

6"

12"

2×6 rafter stock

Cutting line

12" overhang

3½"

Bird's mouth

12"

6"

Rafter length 4'5¼"

Overall length 6'

board at the 12-inch mark. Scribe a cutting line along the short leg.

Next, measure 4 feet, 5¼ inches from that line along the bottom edge of the rafter, and at that point place the square as shown on opposite page. Scribe a short cutting line 1¾ inches along the short leg, then another line perpendicular to the first, 3½ inches long. The 2 lines form a triangular cutout, called the bird's mouth, which fits over the top of the wall plate.

Next, measure 12 inches from the bird's mouth and, using the square held in the 6-inch and 12-inch position, scribe a cutting line for the end of the overhang, which is the portion of the rafter that extends beyond the outside of the shed wall. Cut out the rafter and use it as a pattern for marking the second rafter.

After cutting the 2 rafters, set them in place, with a 1×8 scrap between the tops, to be certain that they fit snugly. If they do, cut the other rafters, using the first one as a pattern. Remember that the 4 rake rafters do not need the bird's-mouth cuts.

Next, cut the ridge to length: 14 feet to include a 1-foot gable overhang at each end. Cut the two 1×8 fascia boards that will cover the rafter ends at the overhangs, or eaves. Cut six 2×4 gable studs on each end, with angled notches to accommodate the rafters. Be sure to cut additional blocks to frame the roof-vent opening.

Lay out the rafter positions on the ridge. The outsides of the rake rafters on the end should be 1 foot from the end of the walls. The other rafters will be 2 feet on center. Cut 2×4 frieze blocks that you will nail between the rafters.

Framing the Roof

You will need another pair of hands to assemble the roof frame. Toenail the gable studs to the cap plate, 16 inches on center, with four 8d nails each, then prop the ridge to its appropriate height with temporary supports.

Start with the rafters that rest on the end walls, toenailing each to the cap plate with three 8d nails and face-nailing them to each gable stud. Continue with the remaining rafters, nailing each to the ridge with two 16d nails; facenail the opposing rafters with two 16d nails. Install the frieze blocks on the top plate as you move along.

Nail collar ties to the rafters, with three 16d nails in each end, to prevent the weight of the roof from spreading the walls. After you nail the fascia boards to the rafters, you can nail the rake rafters to the ends of the ridge board and fascia boards. Predrill for the nails to prevent splitting.

Sheathing and Shingling the Roof

Now it's time to sheath the roof. Nail ½-inch CDX plywood (or OSB) to the rafters, smooth side up, with 6d ring-shank nails, 6 inches on center along the edges and 12 inches on center in the field. Leave 1/16-inch expansion gaps at the ends of panels and ⅛-inch gaps along the edges.

Nail metal drip edge at the eaves. Next, staple 15-pound felt paper horizontally, adding a 12- to 18-inch strip along the eaves for double coverage. Nail the metal drip edge over the felt paper at the edge of the rakes. Finally, apply composition shingles according to manufacturer specifications.

After you complete the shingling, install vents in the gables. If you plan to work in the shed during the winter, install temporary covers over the vents.

Installing the Windows, Doors, and Siding

Apply felt-paper flashing around the window openings, then install the windows. Again, it is useful to have a second pair of hands to help you hold things in place as you nail.

Apply a bead of caulk to the back of the top and side nailing flanges of a window. Then tack one edge of the window to the framing with ¾-inch roofing nails; square the window in the opening by measuring the diagonals and prying gently. When the diagonals are equal, complete the nailing. Now apply sheet-metal flashing across the top of the window.

This shed calls for rough-sawn ⅝-inch plywood siding in 4×8 sheets. Cut openings in the plywood for the door (be sure that the door opening is cut flush with the framing) and windows, allowing for a ⅛-inch gap. Be sure to notch for the rafters.

Before you nail on the siding, staple building paper to the outsides of the studs. Nail the siding to the studs with 8d HDG box nails, placing them 6 inches on center on the edges and 12 inches on center in the field. Note the Z flashing between the top and bottom sheets of plywood at the gable ends. Don't forget to caulk the gap between the windows and the siding before you install the trim.

To build the door, construct a square frame with 2×4s and cover the outside face with plywood siding. Assemble the door on a flat surface, using construction adhesive and nails to hold the plywood to the frame. Hang the door in the opening with butt hinges, and install the handle and hasp on the outside. Add a hook and eye inside if you wish to close the door from within. After caulking around the door, install the trim.

Finishing the Shed

Caulk the corners and install the corner trim. Nail a 1×3 board vertically on one side of each corner, and a 1×4 board on the other side. The wider board covers the edge of the narrow board, making them both look the same size. Prime and paint the shed with an exterior water-based paint, or stain it with a solid, or full-bodied, exterior stain. If the siding is redwood or cedar, and you choose to paint it, use an oil-based primer. Tannins will leach through a water-based primer.

Basic Gable-Roofed Shed Details

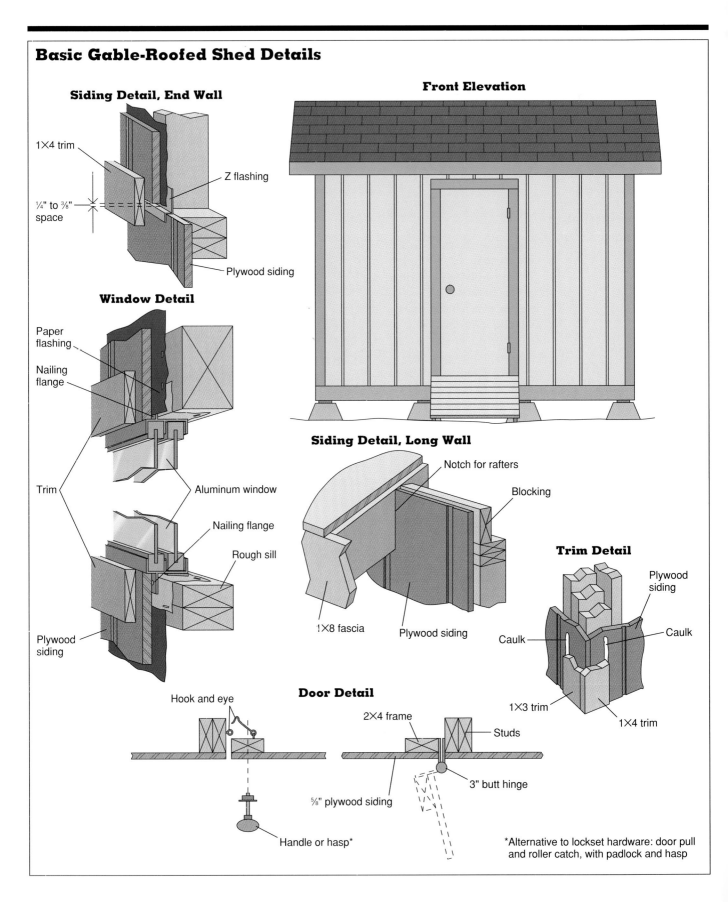

Siding Detail, End Wall

1×4 trim

¼" to ⅜" space

Z flashing

Plywood siding

Window Detail

Paper flashing

Nailing flange

Trim

Aluminum window

Nailing flange

Rough sill

Plywood siding

Front Elevation

Siding Detail, Long Wall

Notch for rafters

Blocking

1×8 fascia

Plywood siding

Trim Detail

Plywood siding

Caulk

Caulk

1×3 trim

1×4 trim

Door Detail

Hook and eye

2×4 frame

Studs

Handle or hasp*

⅝" plywood siding

3" butt hinge

*Alternative to lockset hardware: door pull and roller catch, with padlock and hasp

LEAN-TO POTTING SHED

This shed is economical and relatively simple to build. Because it attaches directly to the side of an existing structure, it has inherent strength. The wide door opening takes advantage of that strength and simplicity to provide easy access. See the Basic Gable-Roofed Shed (page 25) for basic building techniques.

Locating and Laying Out the Shed

This shed has a translucent roof of corrugated plastic. If you orient the shed to the sun, it can serve as a greenhouse as well as a plant-potting and storage area. In any case, select a spot where the shed won't interfere with windows, plumbing, and electrical boxes, wires, or outlets.

Prepare your site to the floor dimensions of the shed (6 feet by 12 feet), pour a slab, and set anchor bolts (see page 22). (If a slab already exists, drill ¾-inch holes 4 inches deep, 16 inches on center, for expansion bolts. If the slab drains poorly or makes an unsuitable floor surface, form and pour a 2-inch-thick concrete topping slab before framing the shed, using stucco wire for the reinforcing mesh.) Another possibility is to build this shed on a deck, in which case you can simply predrill and use lag screws to attach the structure to the decking.

Mark out the length of the shed on the house wall and establish square corners by measuring the diagonals.

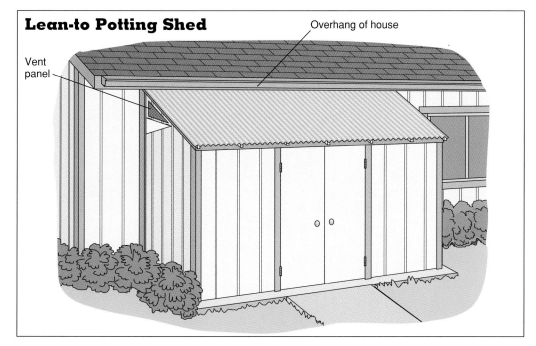

Lean-to Potting Shed

Vent panel · Overhang of house

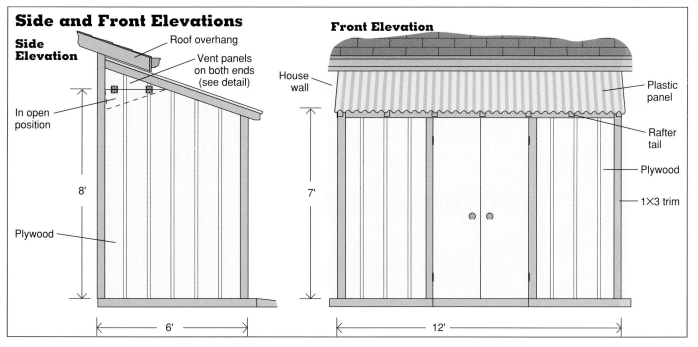

Side and Front Elevations

Side Elevation · Roof overhang · Vent panels on both ends (see detail) · In open position · 8' · Plywood · 6'

Front Elevation · House wall · 7' · 12' · Plastic panel · Rafter tail · Plywood · 1×3 trim

Framing the Walls and Roof

Frame the end walls, raise them into place, and (depending on the foundation) secure the anchors or lag screws firmly. Now plumb the walls and temporarily tack the end studs to the house wall. Secure each end wall into the house framing with four 5/16-inch by 5-inch lag screws, or with expansion bolts if the shed walls don't align with studs.

Frame the front wall with a 48-inch opening for two 24-inch-wide doors, allowing 1¾ inches for the doorjambs. Raise the wall, secure it to the foundation, and nail it to the end walls with 16d HDG common nails, 16 inches apart.

For the roof ledger, cut a 12-foot 2×6 and bevel the top edge for a 4 in 12 roof slope (18 degrees). Position the

Lean-to Potting Shed Materials List

Description	Material/Size	Dimension	Qty
Foundation			
Topping concrete			12 cu ft
Walls & shelves			
Sill plate	2×4 PT	12'	2
Studs & misc	2×4	8'	28
Top plate	2×4	12'	4
Trim boards	1×3	8'	10
Headers	4×4	3'	1
Sheathing (siding)	⅝" CDX ply.	4×8	6
Shelving (work area)	2×8	6'	8
Shelving (plants)	2×10	8'	4
Potting table	2×6 redwood	12'	3
	2×4	6'	5
Rack	1×4	6'	1
Roof			
Ledger	2×6	12'	1
Rafters	2×4	7'	7
Blocking	2×4	12'	4
Corrugated paneling	27" width	8'	6
Closure strips	Corrugated shaped		48 l.f.
Hardware & misc.			
Expansion anchors	½"	10"	10
Toggle bolts	5/16"	4"	8
Lag screws & washers	⅜"	4½"	5
Drip edge	Galvanized	12'	1
Wall vent	Bug screen	24" × 36"	1
Rafter hangers	2×4		7
Neoprene washer screws	1½"		1 box
Caulk			3 tubes
Door hinges	Corrosion resistant		3 pairs
Latch/handle/catch	Your choice		2
Nails & screws	As needed		

Section Through Lean-to Shed

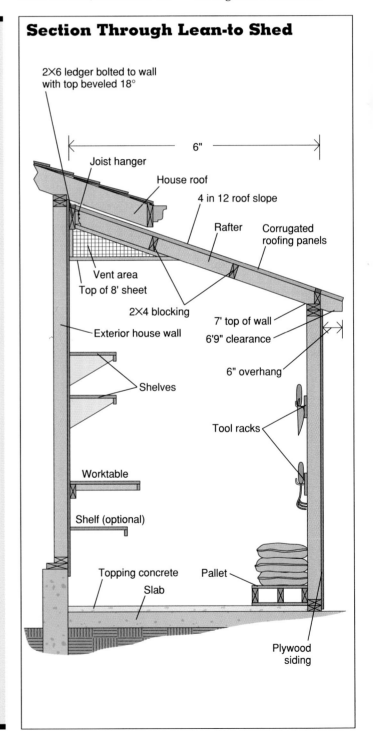

2×6 ledger bolted to wall with top beveled 18°

Joist hanger

House roof

6"

4 in 12 roof slope

Rafter

Corrugated roofing panels

Vent area

Top of 8' sheet

2×4 blocking

7' top of wall

6'9" clearance

Exterior house wall

6" overhang

Shelves

Tool racks

Worktable

Shelf (optional)

Topping concrete

Slab

Pallet

Plywood siding

ledger against the house so that the top edge is 3⅝ inches above the tops of the shed walls where they meet the house wall. You will have to notch out the bottom corners of the ledger to fit over the walls. Secure the ledger to the house framing with ⅜-inch by 5-inch lag screws, 32 inches on center, in a staggered pattern, one bolt per stud. Recess the screw heads.

Next, cut a 2×4 rafter for a 4 in 12 slope. The rafter length is 5 feet, 11¾ inches and the overhang is 6 inches. Test the rafter for fit by placing it along the top of a side wall. Make adjustments, if necessary, and use the rafter as a pattern for cutting six more.

Mark a 24-inch rafter layout along the ledger and front wall plate. Install the rafters by attaching the upper ends to the ledger with joist hangers and the lower ends to the front wall with three 8d nails toe-nailed into each rafter.

Cut 3 sets of 2×4 blocks to fit between the rafters, taking measurements between the rafters for each row of blocking. Bevel the top edges of one set to match the 4 in 12 slope. Install these blocks over the front wall. Install the other 2 rows at 24-inch intervals.

Edge of Roof Detail

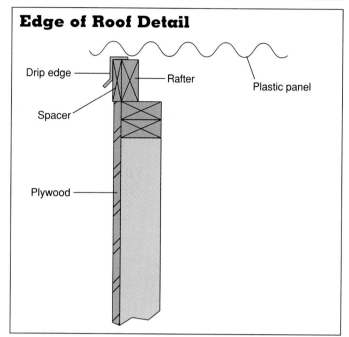

Lean-to Potting Shed

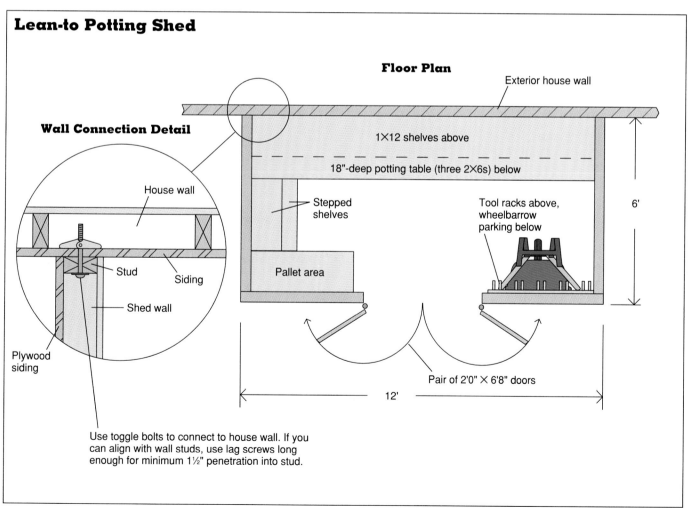

Alternate Connection to House Wall

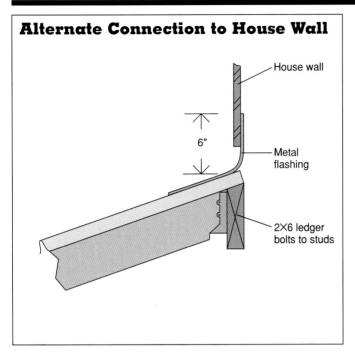

House wall

6"

Metal flashing

2×6 ledger bolts to studs

Vent Panel

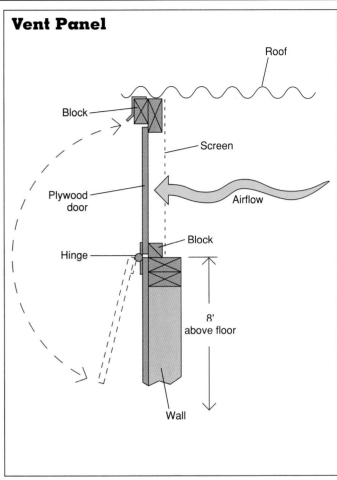

Roof

Block

Screen

Plywood door

Airflow

Hinge

Block

8' above floor

Wall

Nail a 12-foot length of closure strip, which is molding with the corrugated roofing shape cut along the top edge, over the lower row of blocking. Nail another closure strip over the ledger. Before installing the roofing panels, nail metal drip edge to the outside rafters, allowing space between the side of each rafter and the drip edge for the plywood siding that will be installed later.

To install the roofing panels, apply a bead of caulk over each closure strip. Attach the corrugated roofing panels to the closure strips and blocking with 1½-inch galvanized screws and neoprene washers, overlapping the panels according to manufacturer's instructions (usually 2 corrugations). If you can't reach under the eave to attach

the roofing panels to the ledger, tuck a 12-foot 2×4 under the eave to cover the top edge of the panels, then drive screws into it through the panels from below.

See the alternate detail (above) if you're attaching the lean-to to a 2-story wall.

Installing the Siding, Doors, and Trim

Cut the siding to fit and nail it on. The pieces you trim from the end walls to accommodate the slope of the roof should serve as the vent panels. Follow the vent panel detail (above) to construct the vents.

You can build your own door and casing or install a prehung door. When the door is in place, attach the trim as for the Basic Gable-Roofed Shed (see page 25), and caulk all exterior joints.

Organizing the Space

Follow the floor plan and cross section on pages 32 and 33 to organize the interior space to accommodate gardening tools, potting soil, pots of various sizes, gloves, starter trays, and plants. Tool racks can be made of a 1×4 attached to the studs; pairs of 16d common nails can hold shovels, rakes, a hoe, and so forth. A second lower rack can hold shorter tools such as a pick and mattock.

You can build a worktable against the house wall. Use redwood, cedar, or another rot-resistant wood, since you will probably be watering plants inside the shed. Store pots and soil under the table, away from the wet area. Place a small pallet near the door for large bags of potting soil, mulch, and fertilizer. Trowels, gloves, markers, and small bags of gardening materials can sit on upper shelves. Shelves that will hold bottles or jars should have rails, or a small cabinet can be installed to hold breakable items. A set of stepped shelves is a handy place to keep small pots and starter trays.

POOL CABANA

If you have a swimming pool, you have "pool stuff." This cabana is handy because it keeps pool clutter—including wet swimsuits and towels—out of the house. See the Basic Gable-Roofed Shed (page 25) for basic building techniques.

Functional Modules

This design assumes that there is already a patio around or close to the swimming pool, and that the pump and filter are nearby. If you don't have a pool but are planning to install one, this design can help you decide how to configure it in your yard. You can build the cabana on a concrete slab or a wood deck.

The cabana has 3 modules: a storage room, a changing room, and an equipment room. The storage room has shelves both deep and shallow, as well as space for a raft, inner tubes, folding chairs, balls, and pool maintenance equipment. A separate locking cabinet, facing the pool, holds pool chemicals that should be kept out of the reach of children. The changing room has a bench, clothing hooks, and shelves. The 6-foot by 8-foot equipment room gives easy access to the pump and filter for servicing, and removal if necessary. The space may appear too generous, but when you work on the equipment you will find that it is just right.

Pool Cabana

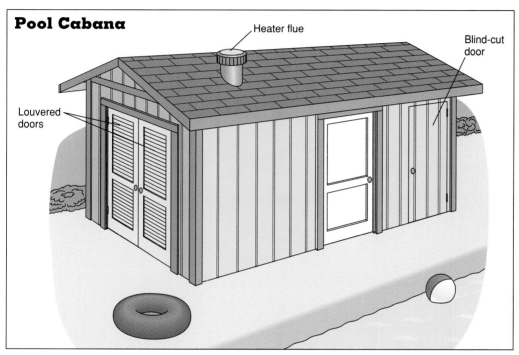

Cabana Shed Elevation

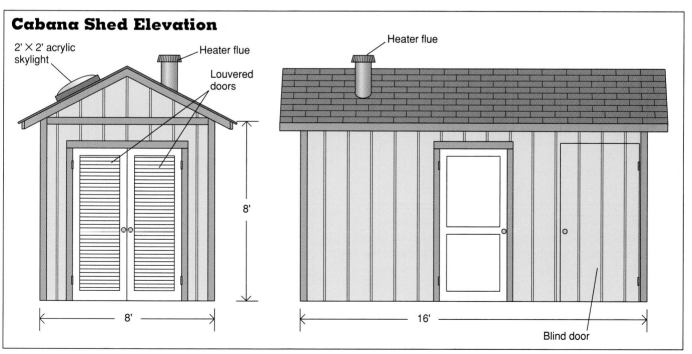

Cabana Floor Plan

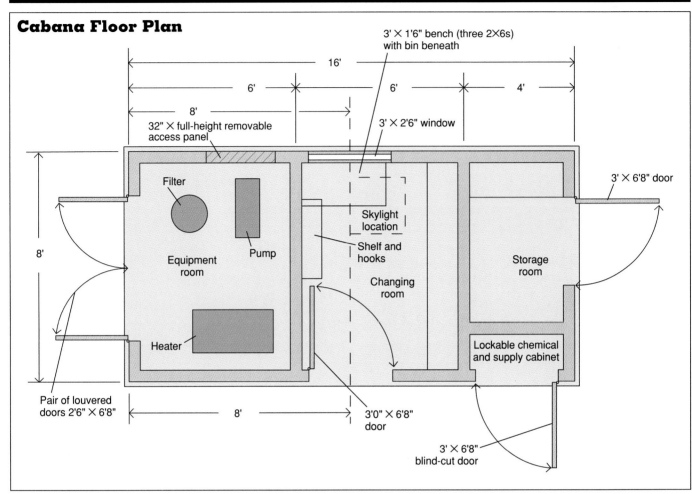

3' × 1'6" bench (three 2×6s) with bin beneath

3' × 2'6" window

32" × full-height removable access panel

16'

6'

6'

4'

8'

8'

Filter

Pump

Equipment room

Heater

Skylight location

Shelf and hooks

Changing room

Storage room

Lockable chemical and supply cabinet

3' × 6'8" door

Pair of louvered doors 2'6" × 6'8"

8'

3'0" × 6'8" door

3' × 6'8" blind-cut door

Framing the Walls

Before framing the walls, form and pour a 2-inch concrete topping slab (see page 22; in place of the 6-inch mesh, use chicken wire supported by small rocks) on the existing 4-inch slab (see right).

Using pressure-treated sill plates, frame standard stud walls with studs 16 inches on center. Skip one stud for the 32-inch access panel on one wall of the equipment room, and add trimmer studs and a header to frame the access panel opening (see illustration on page 38).

When you have framed the walls, raise them and anchor them to the topping slab with ½-inch by 7-inch stainless steel expansion bolts. First, drill ⅝-inch holes through the sill plates at each end and every 4 feet. Then, using a rotary hammer and a bit of the size specified by the bolt manufacturer, drill holes into the concrete to the depth required by the bolts. Blow the debris from the holes with a tire pump.

With the holes in the sill plates aligned over the holes in the slab, drop in the expansion bolts and tighten the nuts. Tack diagonal 1×4 braces to

Floor Detail—Topping Concrete

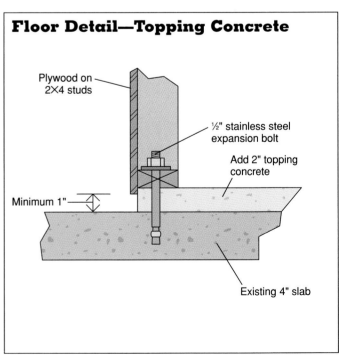

Plywood on 2×4 studs

½" stainless steel expansion bolt

Add 2" topping concrete

Minimum 1"

Existing 4" slab

Pool Cabana Materials List

Description	Material/Size	Dimension	Qty
Foundation			
Concrete slab	Use existing (see page 35)		
Topping concrete	2" thick		21 cu ft
Wall framing			
Sill plates	2×4 PT	16'	4
Studs & misc	2×4	8'	56
Top plates	2×4	16'	8
Headers	4×6	8'	2
	4×6	6'	1
Roof			
Rafters	2×6	6'	22
Collar ties		8'	7
Blocking	2×4	8'	4
Ridge board	1×8	18'	1
Sheathing	½" CDX ply.	4×8	8
Fascia	1×8	12'	3
Underlayment	15-lb felt		200 s.f.
Drip edge	Galvanized	10'	8
Shingles	Composition		200 s.f.
Curb flashing	Aluminum for 2' × 2' opening		1
Skylight	2' × 2' aluminum		1

Materials List (continued)

Description	Material/Size	Dimension	Qty
Finish material			
Exterior siding	⅝" T-111	4×8	13
Window	Sliding aluminum	3'0" × 2'6"	1
Interior plywood	⅜" AC ply.	4x8	8
Shelves	1×12	8'	4
Trim	1×4	8'	16
Paint/stain			2 gal.
Doors			
Changing room & storage room	Panel	3'0" × 6'8"	2
Equipment room	Louvered	2'6" × 6'8"	2
Outside cabinet	Blind cut	3'0" × 6'8"	1
Hardware & misc			
Expansion bolts	½" bolts/ washers	7"	25
Z flashing	Galvanized	10'	2
Framing anchors	Simpson A34 or equiv		4
Nails & screws	As needed		
Door hinges	3"		8 pair
Handle/catch/ lockset			4
Privacy lockset			1

Skylight Detail

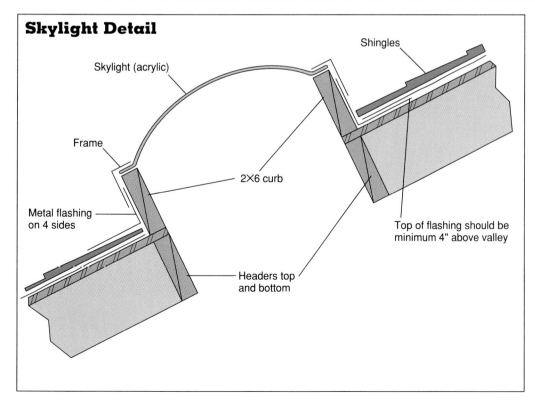

- Skylight (acrylic)
- Frame
- Metal flashing on 4 sides
- 2×6 curb
- Headers top and bottom
- Shingles
- Top of flashing should be minimum 4" above valley

the walls for temporary support while you complete the next step—framing the roof.

Building the Roof

The cabana has a standard gable roof with a 4 in 12 pitch and composition shingles. The rafter length for a 4 in 12 roof is 4 feet 2⅛ inches (allowing for the ridge board). See the Basic Gable-Roofed Shed (page 25) for guidance in building the roof.

Frame the roof with rafters 24 inches on center. Install frieze blocks, leaving one out of each side of the changing room, for ventilation; cover the gaps with screening. Don't forget to frame the 2-foot by

2-foot acrylic skylight and the heater flue if there is one.

Apply the plywood sheathing and 15-pound felt, then carefully flash and caulk the skylight (see detail on page 37) and flue before applying composition shingles.

Installing the Siding, Doors, and Trim

Before you nail on the plywood siding panels, be sure that there is at least 1 inch of clearance between the bottom edges of the plywood and the concrete. The topping slab should give you about 1½ inches. Swimming pools are wet areas, and you don't want the plywood to wick water from a wet patio.

Be sure to leave an unframed opening for the chemical storage cabinet. Blind-cut the plywood for this opening and for the service access panel in the equipment room.

Nail the plywood, including panels for the interior walls, to the studs, with nails 6 inches apart at the edges and 12 inches apart in the field.

Fabricate and hang plywood panel doors for the storage room, changing room, and chemical cabinet. Use louvered doors for the equipment room to provide ventilation. Fabricate the removable panel for access to the pump (see right). Use locking doorknobs for the chemical storage cabinet and the storage room. Finally, nail on the trim, paint or stain the cabana, and go for a swim.

Removable Access Panel

Construction Detail

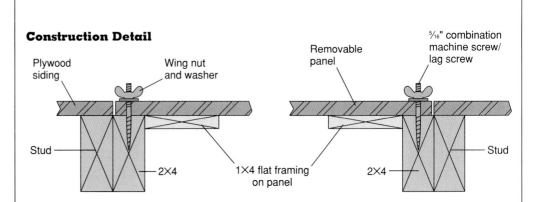

Panel Framing (Interior Face)

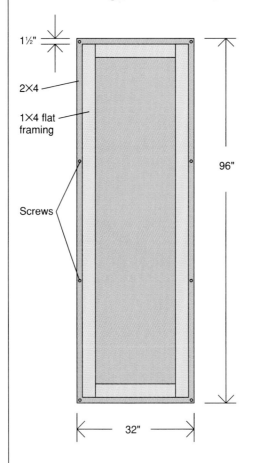

SMALL BARN

This board-and-batten barn is designed for boarding a horse, but you can adapt the design to any purpose. The stall is large enough for a horse to turn around in; the gambrel roof allows plenty of headroom. See the Basic Gable-Roofed Shed (page 25) for basic building techniques.

Building the Foundation

Select a well-drained site, level it, and lay out string lines for the perimeter of the barn. Dig 14 holes along the perimeter for the 18-inch-square concrete footings, 4 feet on center, a minimum of 12 inches deep or to the frost line. Dig 2 more holes for 2 footings for the interior partition wall.

Build 8-inch-high forms for a strip footing, or grade beam, which will provide a curb above the ground. The forms should be 6 inches apart and level. They should run continuously around the perimeter, except at the door openings, and cross over the footing holes. Where the forms stop for a door opening, nail a scrap of plywood or 2-by material across the ends of the form boards to make a dam. Build forms for the interior partition wall as well.

Next, suspend No. 4 rebar between the forms, 1½ inches from the top edge of the forms. Unlike the rebar for conventional perimeter foundations, the rebar for this strip footing should not be a continuous, unbroken piece. Instead, there should be a 6-inch gap in the rebar over every footing hole so that the rebar does not interfere with placement of the post anchors after the concrete is poured. This means that the rebar will be a series of 42-inch lengths with 6-inch gaps between them.

For each footing hole, wire a grid of four 12-inch lengths of rebar, two in each direction, and place it 3 inches above the bottom of the hole.

Fill the footing holes and forms with concrete and screed it level. Then, set a post anchor directly over each footing, centered laterally and aligned with the outside edge of the strip footing. The anchors must be accurately aligned in both directions so that the posts will be square to one another. Also place 2 anchor bolts between post anchors, except at door openings, within 12 inches of the anchors.

Framing the Walls

After the concrete has set for at least 24 hours, erect the 4×4 corner posts and bolt them to the post anchors. Temporarily brace them diagonally with 2×4s. Cut one post to 7 feet, 8-inches; using a builder's level, water level, or long straightedge and carpenter's level, mark the other posts even with the cut one; trim them all.

Set the long 4×8 beams on the posts and fasten them with post caps or other suitable steel connectors. Now install the intermediate posts, cutting them to fit between the post anchors and beams. Next, install wall bracing strips diagonally at one end of each long wall, so that each strip spans 3 posts (two 4-foot bays). Nail bracing to both the exterior and interior sides of the posts.

Finally, install the 3 short 4×8 beams. Trim them so that they fit between the long beams, then connect them to the long beams with steel beam hangers.

Small Barn

Small Barn Floor Plan

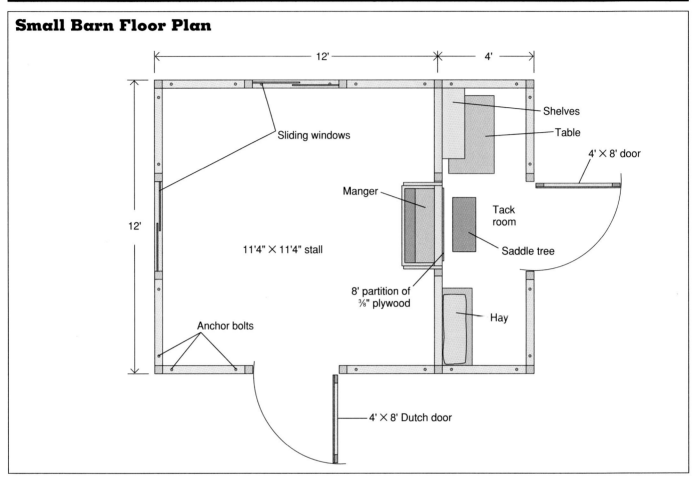

12'

12'

4'

Sliding windows

Shelves

Table

4' × 8' door

Manger

Tack room

Saddle tree

11'4" × 11'4" stall

8' partition of ⅜" plywood

Hay

Anchor bolts

4' × 8' Dutch door

Elevations

End Wall

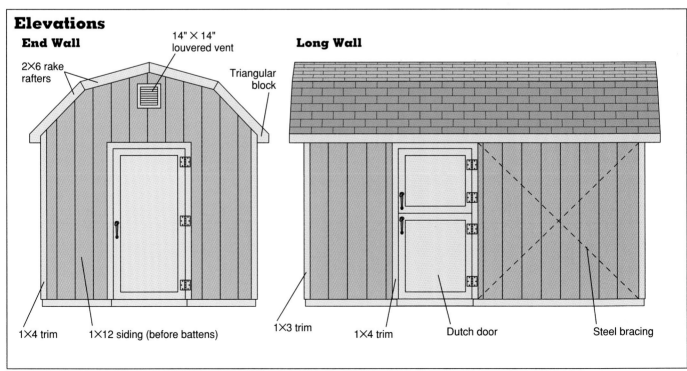

2×6 rake rafters

14" × 14" louvered vent

Triangular block

1×4 trim

1×12 siding (before battens)

Long Wall

1×3 trim

1×4 trim

Dutch door

Steel bracing

Bolt sill plates to the foundation between the posts except at the 2 doors. Toenail 3 rows of horizontal nailers between the posts, 24 inches on center. As you do this, frame window openings high on the walls, just below the beams, 44½ inches long and 16 inches high, to let in natural light. Leave 2 bays open—one in the stall and one in the tack room—for doors. Install a 4×6 header over each doorway and attach it to the posts with beam hangers.

Building the Roof

Referring to the Gambrel Roof Truss Detail on page 44, fabricate 9 built-up trusses with 2×6s and ½-inch plywood. Before starting, measure between the outside edges of the wall beams to be sure that they are 12 feet apart. If not, adjust the truss dimensions so that the distance between the vertical cuts of the bird's-mouth notches is the same as the distance between the outside edges of the wall beams.

Attach the plywood with construction adhesive and 1¼-inch deck screws. On the 2 end trusses install a 2×4 horizontal nailer, as shown, sandwiching it between the plywood gussets. Use scraps of ½-inch plywood as furring material to build up the nailer and the lower portion of the truss members so that the siding boards will have solid backing.

Small Barn Materials List

Description	Material/Size	Dimension	Qty
Foundation			
Concrete	Varies		Approx 1.8 cu yd
Reinforcing steel	#4 rebar	20'	6
Sand			2.4 cu yd
Wall framing			
Posts	4×4	8'	16
Beams	4×8	16'	2
		12'	3
Headers	4×6	8'	1
Sill plates	2×4 PT	8'	8
Nailers	2×4	8'	12
	2×2	18'	2
Roof			
Truss chords	2×6	8'	9
		10'	9
Rake rafters	2×6	8'	2
		10'	2
Gussets	½" CDX ply.	4×8	7
Blocking, nailers	4×4	10'	6
	2×4	10'	6
Fascia	2×8	18'	2
Sheathing	½" CDX ply.	4×8	4
		4×10	4
Underlayment	15-lb felt		288 s.f.
Drip edge	Galvanized	10'	7
Shingles	Composition		288 s.f.
Ridge cap shingles	Composition		18 l.f.
Exterior finish			
Siding	1×12	8'	34
		12'	26
Windows	Aluminum sliders	3'8" × 1'4"	2
Soffit nailer	2×2	18'	2
Soffit	½" ply. or equiv	6" × 18'	2
Battens	1×2	8'	64
Trim	1×4	8'	9
	1×3	8'	4
	1×2	8'	10
Wood doors	2×4	8'	10
	1×12	8'	8
Paint/stain			2 gal.

Materials List (continued)

Description	Material/Size	Dimension	Qty
Interior finish			
Interior wall	⅜" CDX ply.	4×8	3
Corral boards	2×8	12'	36
Manger	2×4	6'	2
	2×8	6'	2
	2×12	6'	1
Tack-room shelving	1×12	8'	5
Hardware & misc			
Tie wire for rebar	Small roll		1
Anchor bolts	½" dia	10"	30
Post anchors	Simpson BC4 or equiv		16
Wall bracing straps	Simpson B126 or equiv	11'	4
Post caps	Simpson PC44 or equiv		10
Corner beam connectors	Simpson RTC44 or equiv		4
Beam hangers	For interior beam	4×8	2
Beam hangers	Concealed flange	4×6	4
Framing anchors	Simpson A34 or equiv		32
Vents	Louvered	14" × 14"	2
Lockset or gate latch			3 ea
Hinges	4"		7
Nails & screws	As needed		

Before erecting the trusses, cut shaped 4×4 blocks to fit between the trusses, three for each bay. The 2 bevels at the top of each block are 15-degree angles. Cut 18 blocks 21½ inches long for the 6 interior bays. The blocks for the end trusses are longer because they also support the roof overhang. Cut the 3 blocks for the first truss at 34½ inches, and the 3 blocks for the final truss at 32 inches. Cut notches in the 2 end trusses to let in these blocks, which are called lookouts or outriggers.

Erecting the trusses requires 3 people. Start at one end, installing the first truss so that the outside face of the plywood is flush with the outside face of the wall framing. Brace this truss with temporary diagonal braces and with temporary cleats nailed to the outside faces of the posts and beam. Toenail each end of

Barn Cross Section

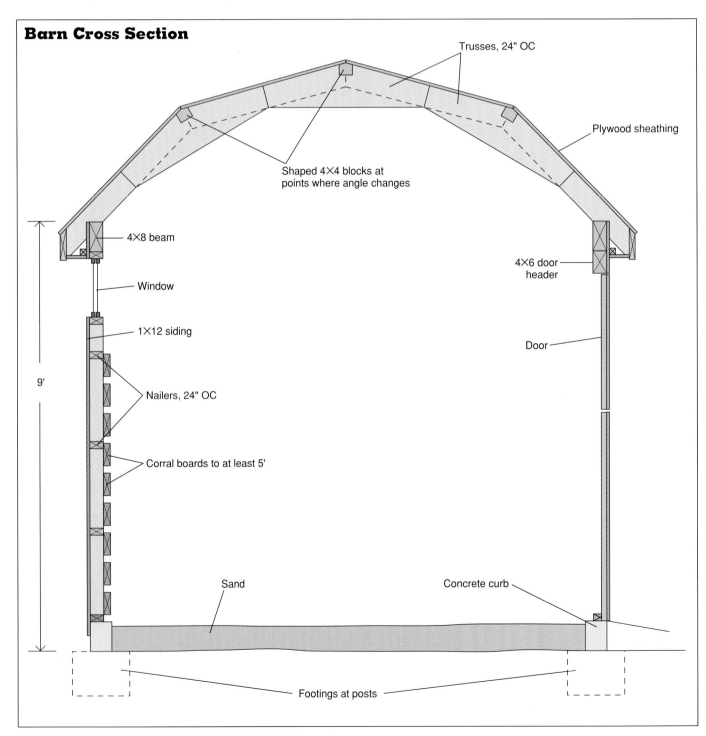

Trusses, 24" OC

Plywood sheathing

Shaped 4×4 blocks at points where angle changes

4×8 beam

Window

1×12 siding

4×6 door header

Door

Nailers, 24" OC

Corral boards to at least 5'

9'

Sand

Concrete curb

Footings at posts

each truss to the wall beams with three 8d nails. Install the blocks between each pair of trusses as you go.

When all of the trusses have been erected, reinforce the toenailed connections with framing anchors. Install 2×4 blocking between the trusses along the tops of the wall beams. Attach 2×8 fascia boards, with 45-degree beveled tops, to the outside edges of the trusses; the boards should extend 10½ inches beyond each end wall (12 inches if you miter the corner—read on).

To install the 2×6 rake rafters for the 2 overhangs, cut the top 2 rafters the same as the top 2 chords of the truss pattern and install them first. Then, cut the upper angle for each lower piece, hold the piece in place, and mark the lower cutting line where the outside face of the fascia board intersects it. (For a spectacular display of carpentry skill, cut this line on a 45-degree bevel—a compound bevel cut—then trim the end of the fascia board with an identical bevel, so that the 2 cuts create a miter joint.) Nail the board in place and nip off the bottom.

Install ½-inch CDX plywood sheathing over the trusses, which are designed to accommodate full-width sheets. Cut each 4×10 sheet into 2 shorter lengths of approximately 37¼ inches and 82¾ inches (take field measurements first).

After installing the sheathing, apply metal drip edge, 15-pound felt paper, and shingles, according to manufacturer specifications.

Installing the Siding and Trim

After installing the windows (see page 29), install the 1×12 siding boards. Nail each board with two 8d HDG nails at the soleplate, each nailer, and each beam.

Using a 14-inch by 14-inch louvered vent as a pattern, cut a vent opening near the peak of each end wall. Install the vent.

Next, install the 2×2 nailers for the soffits. The bottoms should be level with the bottoms of the rafter tails, and the ends should extend 10½ inches beyond the end wall framing.

Cut and install ½-inch plywood for the soffits. Box in the ends of the soffits with filler pieces cut from scraps of siding or plywood. Cut a triangular piece of 2-by lumber for the end of each soffit where it's not covered by the rake rafter. Attach it to the 2×2 nailer and the rake rafter with construction adhesive and 3-inch deck screws; predrill for the screws.

Nail the 1×2 battens over the siding joints with 6d HDG box nails. If the siding is unseasoned, nail the battens on one side only to prevent the battens from splitting when the siding boards shrink as they dry; after a couple of months nail the other side.

Trim each corner of the barn with a 1×3 nailed to the side wall and a 1×4 nailed to the end wall, lapping the edge of the 1×3. Trim the window and door openings with 1x4s; trim the louvered vents with 1×2s.

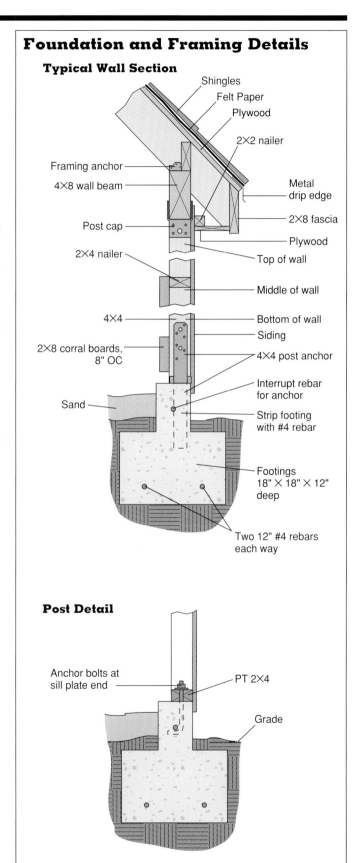

Foundation and Framing Details

Typical Wall Section

Shingles
Felt Paper
Plywood
2×2 nailer
Framing anchor
4×8 wall beam
Metal drip edge
Post cap
2×8 fascia
Plywood
2×4 nailer
Top of wall
Middle of wall
4×4
Bottom of wall
Siding
2×8 corral boards, 8" OC
4×4 post anchor
Interrupt rebar for anchor
Sand
Strip footing with #4 rebar
Footings 18" × 18" × 12" deep
Two 12" #4 rebars each way

Post Detail

Anchor bolts at sill plate end
PT 2×4
Grade

Gambrel Roof Truss Detail

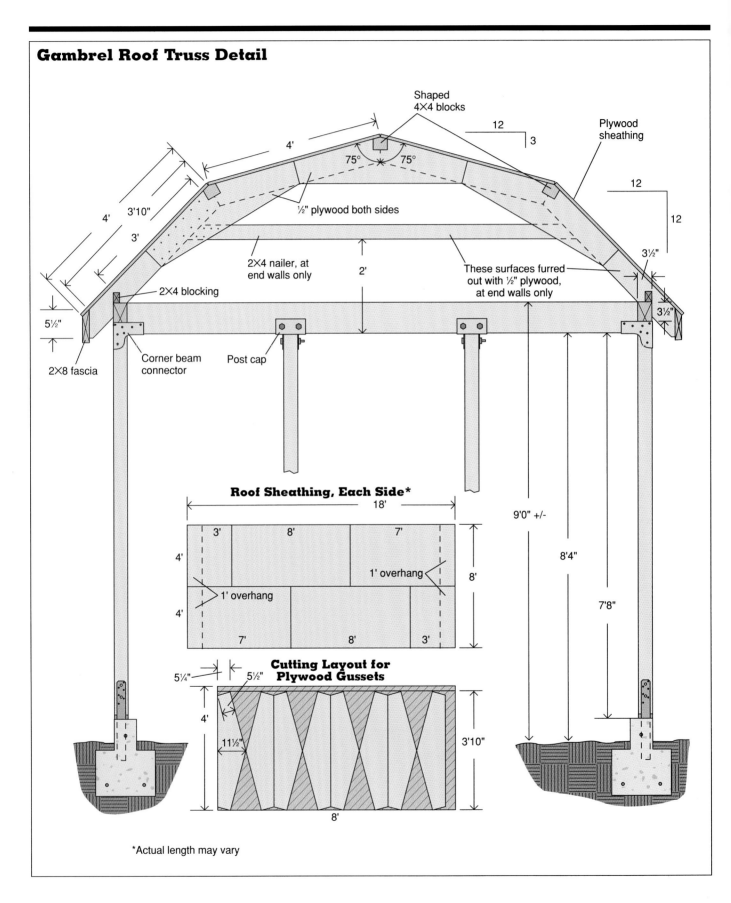

Shaped 4×4 blocks

Plywood sheathing

4'

75° 75°

12
3

12

12

3'10"

4'

3

½" plywood both sides

3½"

2×4 nailer, at end walls only

2'

These surfaces furred out with ½" plywood, at end walls only

5½"

3½"

2×4 blocking

2×8 fascia

Corner beam connector

Post cap

9'0" +/-

8'4"

7'8"

Roof Sheathing, Each Side*

18'

3'   8'   7'

4'

1' overhang

8'

1' overhang

4'

7'   8'   3'

Cutting Layout for Plywood Gussets

5¼"   5½"

4'

11½"

3'10"

8'

*Actual length may vary

Finishing the Interior

Separate the tack room from the stall with an 8-foot-high partition of ⅜-inch plywood on a simple stud wall erected between the posts. If you wish, you can finish the other tack-room walls with plywood or boards.

Inside the stall, nail 2×8s to the posts to a height of at least 5 feet, to serve as corral boards. Horses are lovely animals but they are large and very strong. Corral boards will protect the partition and exterior siding from kicks and the rubbing that horses love to do. Leave no more than a 2-inch space between these boards, so the horse's hooves don't get stuck between them. You will need at least 6 boards on each wall.

Place 3 to 4 inches of sand on the floor of the horse stall. For the tack-room floor, place 4 inches of crushed rock, instead of sand, for more secure footing.

In the tack room, build a simple tree for the saddle. To hang bridles and other gear, use a rack with nails. For smaller items, attach a simple set of shelves to the wall; if you face the shelves with cabinet doors, everything will look tidy. A plain wood pallet serves quite well for hay and grain storage.

Provide a place for water in the horse stall. For hay and grain, follow the diagram below to build a manger. It is supported with diagonal 2×4s that attach to the posts and rest on the curb. Without that support, the horse would knock down the manger.

Building the Doors

Each part of this barn has its own door. For the stall, follow the detail at right to build a Dutch door, which consists of 1×12s over an X frame of 2×4s. The tack room has a single door constructed in similar X-frame fashion.

Each door opening is approximately 44 inches wide and 7 feet, 8 inches high. When the doors are ready, hang them on the building with strap hinges.

Dutch Door Detail

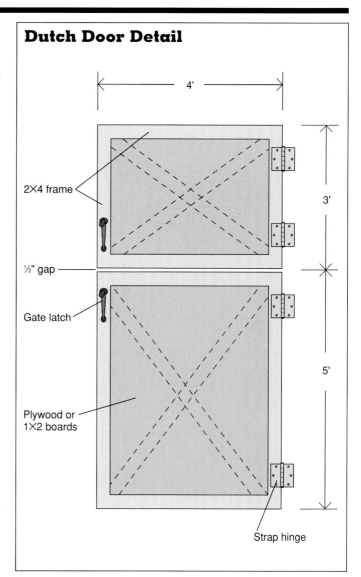

2×4 frame

½" gap

Gate latch

Plywood or 1×2 boards

Strap hinge

4'

3'

5'

Manger and Tack Room Interior

Manger

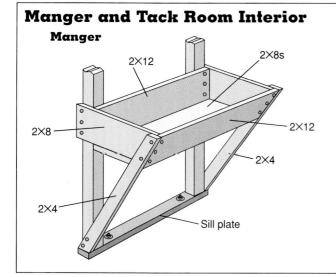

2×12
2×8s
2×8
2×12
2×4
2×4
Sill plate

Tack Room

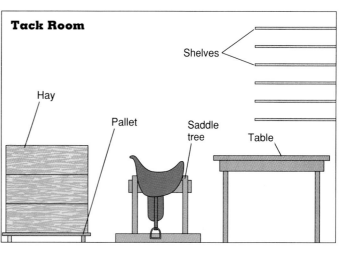

Shelves
Hay
Pallet
Saddle tree
Table

MORE COMPLEX SHEDS

Not all sheds are modest, utilitarian structures. Some are more like barns, with enough space to store several vehicles, a small herd of livestock, or all of the equipment for a small business. Others are decorative buildings intended to grace the landscape as much as to provide shelter. The four sheds in this chapter are superb examples of how a shed can be much more than basic storage. Each design is an interesting building, with a thoughtful interplay between overall proportions, structural details, and finishing touches. Three of the designs—the Utility Barn, the Japanese-Style Shed, and the Gazebo Office/Storage—have intriguing structural systems that differ from conventional light-frame construction. The fourth design, patterned after an English Tudor cottage, is simply a variation on the Basic Gable-Roofed Shed presented in the preceding chapter.

A custom-built shed offers scope to the imagination as well as storage space. This shed, as distinctive as the four designs presented in this chapter, shares many of their qualities: It has a nice sense of proportion and scale; the roof is an interesting interplay of angles and planes; many of the materials are of home-construction quality; and it features lots of windows.

UTILITY BARN

This utility barn is for people who need a large space for a vehicle and a workshop, with plenty of additional room for storage. The design calls for a concrete slab foundation and uses post-and-beam construction, with a double roof. Metal fasteners for support are augmented by extensive bracing to enhance overall shear strength.

Building the Foundation

The slab foundation has a continuous perimeter footing. Note that it will need to be centered under the 2 posts at each end of the barn. In addition, there are footings for the 6 interior posts, 18 inches by 18 inches and dug to a depth of at least 18 inches (see detail below left).

In earthquake country the post anchors should have long enough brackets to prevent the posts from cracking at the base. You will need to set and orient the anchor bolts and post anchors perfectly to ensure straight, plumb framing. Orient the 4 end post anchors so that the sill plates can be set between the brackets.

Framing the Walls

At least 2 people are required to frame the walls and roof. Have sturdy ladders on hand, work carefully, and brace each wall securely before proceeding to the next. Frame the low outside walls first. Cut the studs to 5 feet, 7½ inches. Use pressure-treated 2×4s for the sill plates.

Working on the ground, drill holes for the anchor bolts, lay out the 16-inch stud spacing on the sill and top plates, and assemble the walls. The cap plate should be 3½ inches shorter than the top plate at each end. After you tilt up the walls, brace them plumb with scrap 2×4s.

Next, install the posts for the center bay. Avoid "boxed heart" pieces, which are cut from the center of the tree and have a distinctive bull's-eye grain pattern on the end; they twist and crack easily. Bolt the posts to the post anchors, plumb them, and brace them securely.

Foundation Layout and Floor Plan

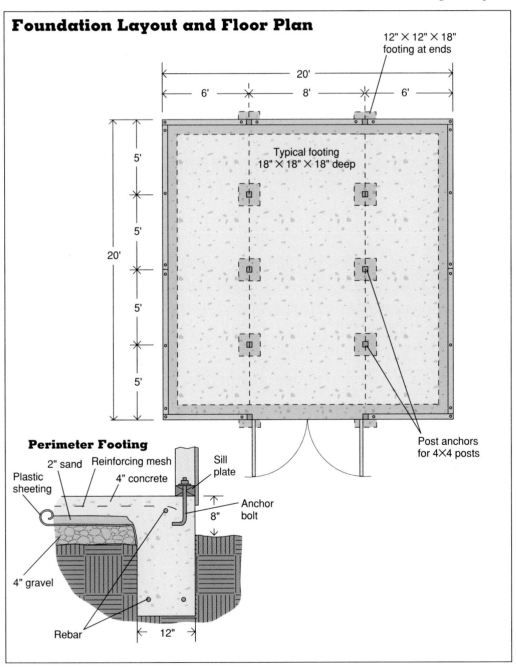

20'

6' 8' 6'

12" × 12" × 18" footing at ends

Typical footing 18" × 18" × 18" deep

5' 5' 5' 5'

20'

Post anchors for 4×4 posts

Perimeter Footing

2" sand
Plastic sheeting
Reinforcing mesh
4" concrete
Sill plate
Anchor bolt
8"
4" gravel
Rebar
12"

48

Utility Barn

Building Frame and Sequence of Construction

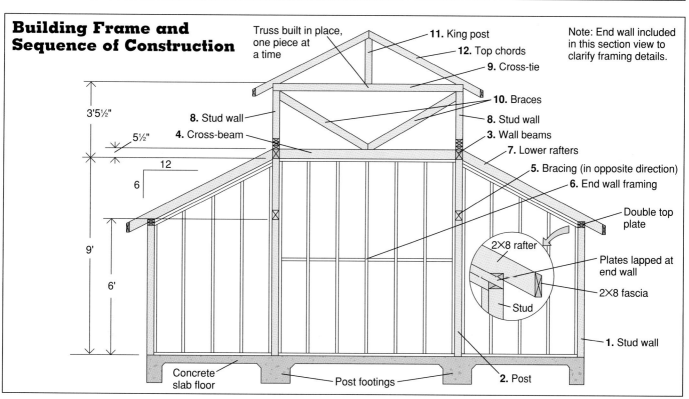

Truss built in place, one piece at a time

11. King post
12. Top chords
9. Cross-tie

Note: End wall included in this section view to clarify framing details.

8. Stud wall
4. Cross-beam

10. Braces
8. Stud wall
3. Wall beams
7. Lower rafters
5. Bracing (in opposite direction)
6. End wall framing

Double top plate

2×8 rafter

Plates lapped at end wall

2×8 fascia

Stud

1. Stud wall

3'5½"
5½"
12
6
9'
6'

Concrete slab floor
Post footings
2. Post

Long Section

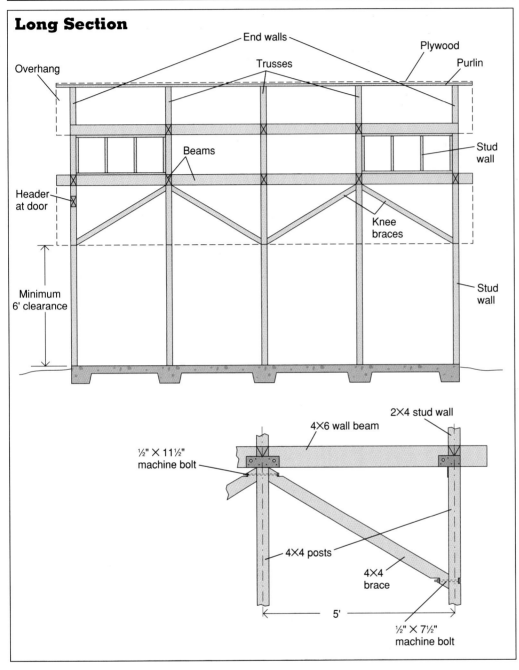

Long Section labels:
- Overhang
- End walls
- Trusses
- Plywood
- Purlin
- Beams
- Stud wall
- Header at door
- Knee braces
- Stud wall
- Minimum 6' clearance

Detail labels:
- ½" × 11½" machine bolt
- 4×6 wall beam
- 2×4 stud wall
- 4×4 posts
- 4×4 brace
- 5'
- ½" × 7½" machine bolt

Mark one post 9 feet above the floor; then, using a water level or string level, mark the rest of the posts at the same height. Trim them and install a post cap on top of each post.

Set the 4×6 beams on top, overhanging each end by at least 12 inches (to support the upper ends of the rake rafters). Make sure that the distance between the top of the posts matches the distance between them at the base; then, nail the brackets to the beam. Attach beam hangers for the five 4×6 cross-beams along the inside of each beam where it rests on the posts, then install the cross-beams.

To provide additional shear strength between the posts, install 4×4 knee braces (see above). Bolt these to the posts with ½-inch machine bolts, nuts, and malleable washers.

Next, frame the middle section of the back wall under the cross-beam; use a single top plate. Except for the 2 end studs, lay out the studs on a 16-inch pattern that starts at one of the building corners. Install blocking between the studs, 48 inches above the floor.

For the front wall, hang the 4×8 door header between the posts so that the bottom is 7 feet, 6 inches above the floor, then fill in a short wall above it. Again, use a single top plate, and lay out the studs on a pattern that starts at one of the building corners.

Next, frame the 2 sloping sections of each end wall. First, measure and cut the sill plate. Determine the top plate length by measuring the distance between the bottom of the wall beam and the top of the side wall. Each end of the plate should be cut at a 26½-degree angle (6 in 12 roof slope).

Next, holding this plate in place (use scraps of 2×4 as spacers for the cap plate), measure down from each end to the floor to determine the length of the 2 outside studs. Mark and cut two 2×4s to these lengths, subtracting 1½ inches for the sill plate and cutting the tops at the roof angle.

Nail together these 2 studs, the sill plate, and the top plate. Test the frame for fit, lay it on the floor, and fill in the rest of the studs on a 16-inch layout that starts at the same building corner as the layout for the other studs in this wall.

Erect the wall section, then cut and install the cap plate. It should overlap the top plate of the side wall, so you'll have to bevel the side wall top plate to accommodate the slope. If everything fits correctly, the 2 cap plates will be flush at the inside corner where they meet.

End View

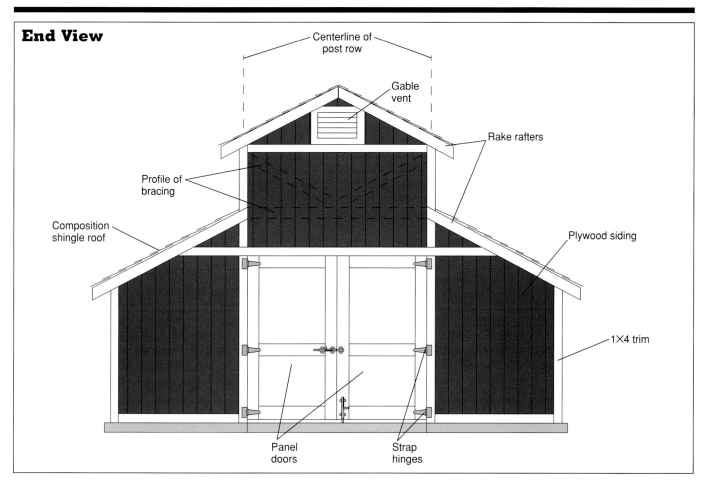

Centerline of post row

Gable vent

Rake rafters

Profile of bracing

Composition shingle roof

Plywood siding

1×4 trim

Panel doors

Strap hinges

Side View

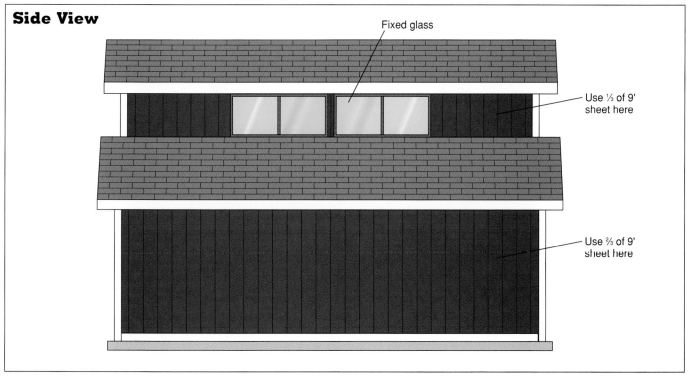

Fixed glass

Use ⅓ of 9' sheet here

Use ⅔ of 9' sheet here

Utility Barn Materials List

Description	Material/Size	Dimension	Qty
Foundation			
Rock			4.4 cu yd
Concrete	5-sack mix		10.5 cu yd
Reinforcing steel	#4 rebar	20'	8
	#4 rebar	12"	40
Wire mesh	6✕6/10,10		400 s.f.
Sand			2.2 cu yd
Moisture barrier	Polyethylene film	6 mil	400 s.f.
Dobie blocks		2"	100
Wall framing			
Posts	4✕4	9'	10
Wall beams	4✕6	12'	4
Door header	4✕8	8'	1
Sill plates	2✕4 PT	10'	8
Top, cap & soleplates	2✕4	10'	32
Studs & misc	2✕4	12'	36
	2✕4	8'	28
Braces	4✕4	6'	10
Roof			
Rafters	2✕6	8'	26
Blocking	2✕4	10'	4
Cross-beams	4✕6	8'	3
Purlins	2✕4	12'	16
Blocking	2✕6	10'	4
Truss posts, king posts	4✕4	10'	3
Truss cross-ties	4✕4	8'	3
Truss rafter chords	4✕4	12'	3
Fascia	2✕8	12'	8
Truss gussets	¾" AC ply.	4✕8	1
Sheathing	½" AC ply.	4✕8	24
Underlayment	15-lb felt		616 s.f.
Shingles	Composition		616 s.f.
Drip edge	Galvanized	10'	5
Ridge flashing			20'
Exterior finish			
Windows	Aluminum fixed	4'0" ✕ 2'0"	4
Siding	½" ply.	4✕9	10
Trim	1✕4	12'	10
	1✕4	8'	2
Doors, field built	1✕6	8'	14
Paint/stain	As needed		

Materials List (continued)

Description	Material/Size	Dimension	Qty
Hardware & misc			
Anchor bolts	½"	10"	22
Post anchors	Simpson CB44 or equiv		10
Post caps	Simpson PC44 or equiv		10
Rafter hangers	2✕6		22
Framing anchors	Simpson A34 or equiv		36
Beam hangers	4✕6		10
Post caps (for truss)	4✕4		6
Nailing plates	4✕8		12
Nails & screws	As needed		
Reinforcing straps	2" ✕ 12"		18
Machine bolts, nuts & washers		½" ✕ 6"	21
		½" ✕ 7½"	10
		½" ✕ 11½"	6
Flashing, various	Aluminum roll	6"	50 l.f.
Gable vents	Louvered	24" ✕ 18"	2
Building paper		36" roll	2
Hinges, T or strap	Heavy duty		6
Spring latches			2
Hasp			1
Cane bolts			2

Building the Lower Roof

Frame the lower roofs first; they will serve as platforms for the upper walls and trusses. The roof slope is 6 in 12. Using a framing square, start the layout for the first rafter by marking the plumb cut for the upper end. Measure 6 feet, 6⁶⁄₁₆ inches from that mark along the bottom of the rafter and mark the plumb cut for the bird's mouth; finish the bird's mouth with a 3½-inch seat cut. Measure another 13⅜ inches beyond the bird's mouth to mark the plumb cut for the overhang. Cut out this rafter, test it to fit, and use it as a pattern for the others (but do not cut bird's mouths in the 4 end rafters and the 4 rake rafters).

To install the rafters, nail rafter hangers to the wall beams, 24 inches on center, with the first and last hangers flush with the outside edges of the end walls. Mark a corresponding 24-inch layout along the top plate. Set the top end of each rafter into the rafter hanger, toenail the bird's mouth to the top plate with three 8d nails, then nail the top end to the rafter hanger.

Roof Framing Plan

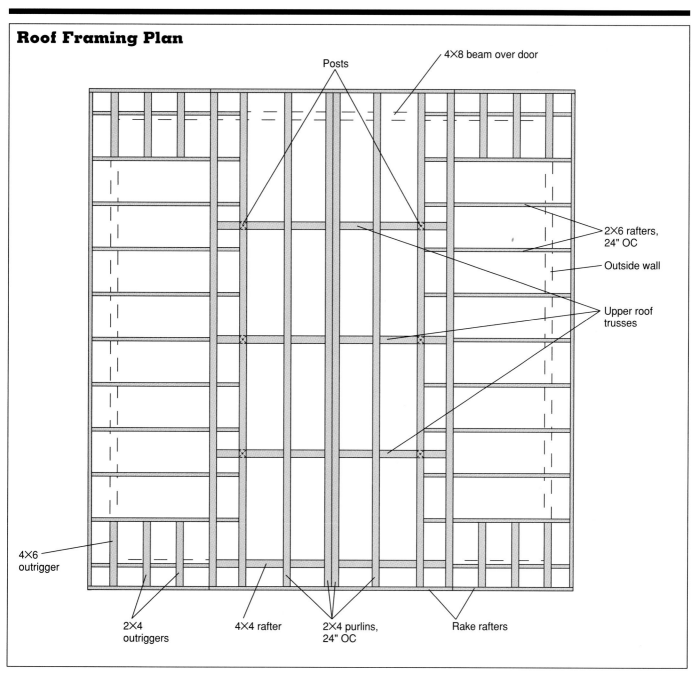

Posts

4×8 beam over door

2×6 rafters, 24" OC

Outside wall

Upper roof trusses

4×6 outrigger

2×4 outriggers

4×4 rafter

2×4 purlins, 24" OC

Rake rafters

Next, notch the end rafters for the 2×4 outriggers, 24 inches on center. Nail the outriggers with 16d nails. The outriggers should extend 12 inches beyond the wall.

Nail the rake rafters (no bird's mouths) to the outriggers. Nail frieze blocks between the rafters along the top of the side walls. Nail 2×8 fascia boards, with the tops beveled at 26½ degrees, to the rafter tails. Finally, install plywood sheathing with 8d common nails, 6 inches apart at the edges and 12 inches in the field. Stagger the vertical joints 4 feet, and leave ⅛-inch expansion gaps at the ends of sheets.

Building the Upper Roof

The truss system is designed to be built in place. For temporary scaffolding, nail planks across the 4×6 cross-beams.

Build the upper sections of the end walls first. Cut the soleplates 8 feet, 3½ inches long so that they overlap both wall beams (see page 54, bottom). Each wall is 3 feet tall at the ends and 4 feet, 11 inches high at the peak, including the soleplate and a single top plate. Frame openings for the louvered vents and install the vents by nailing the flanges to the framing around the openings. (Some types of vents, without the nailing

53

Truss Detail

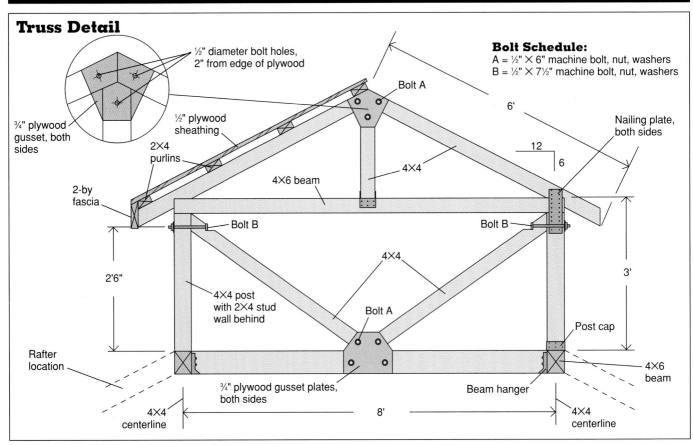

½" diameter bolt holes, 2" from edge of plywood

¾" plywood gusset, both sides

½" plywood sheathing

2×4 purlins

2-by fascia

Bolt A

4×4

4×6 beam

Bolt B

Bolt B

Bolt Schedule:
A = ½" × 6" machine bolt, nut, washers
B = ½" × 7½" machine bolt, nut, washers

6'

Nailing plate, both sides

12

6

3'

4×4

2'6"

4×4 post with 2×4 stud wall behind

Bolt A

Post cap

4×6 beam

Rafter location

¾" plywood gusset plates, both sides

Beam hanger

8'

4×4 centerline

4×4 centerline

End Wall: Upper Frame

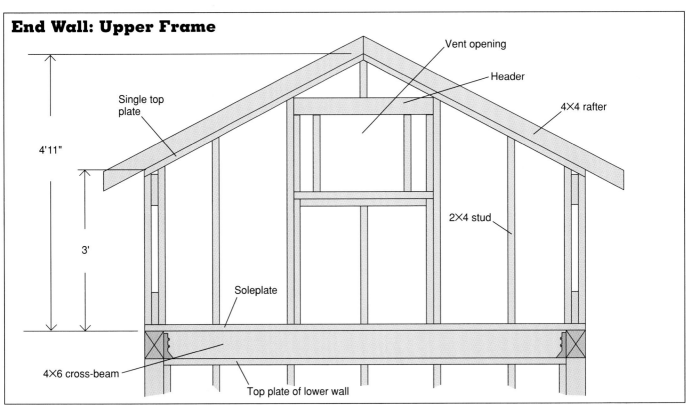

Vent opening

Header

4×4 rafter

Single top plate

4'11"

2×4 stud

3'

Soleplate

4×6 cross-beam

Top plate of lower wall

flanges, are intended to be installed after the siding is in place.)

Next, erect 32½-inch 4×4 posts above the 6 interior posts (see page 54, top). Install the 4×4 cross-ties over the posts.

Frame 2×4 walls between the posts; frame the rough openings for the windows with built-up curbs and a 2×4 plate above the opening. Be sure the windows will fit in the rough openings. Attach them to the posts with 4" by 8" nailing plates, one on each side of each post.

Cut gussets out of ¾-inch plywood, bolt them to the lower 4×6 cross beams, and install the diagonal braces.

Now attach the king posts to the centers of the cross-ties. Cut the top truss chords the same way as you would rafters, and bolt them to the king posts with plywood gussets; attach them to the side posts with nailing plates. Install 2×6 blocking between the trusses above the top plates. Finally, nail 2-inch by 12-inch reinforcing straps across all of the truss posts to connect the top plates together.

To complete the roof, nail 2×4 purlins, 24 inches on center, along the length of the roof; they should extend 12 inches beyond each end wall. Attach beveled fascia boards to the ends of the rafters, overhanging the end wall 12 inches. Nail 2×6 rake rafters to the fascia boards and purlins. The tops of the rake rafters should be flush with the tops of the purlins and fascia boards. Use caution when installing these rafters, because of the height. You should have at least one helper and a safety rope. Install ½-inch plywood sheathing, with the long edges running across the purlins.

Installing the Roofing and Drip Edge

Starting with the upper roof, apply drip edge and 2 layers of 15-pound felt paper over the sheathing. Cover that with shingles according to manufacturer specifications.

When you finish shingling each lower roof section, install L flashing across the top of the last row of shingles where they abut the upper wall framing. Nail the upper half of the flashing to the wall framing, and bend it so that the bottom half lies flat on the roof. The upper half will be covered by the plywood siding, which should be installed with at least ¼ inch of clearance between the flashing and the bottom of the siding.

Installing the Windows and Siding

Simple windows with fixed glass and aluminum frames are sufficient for this shed in most climates, but openable windows will provide needed ventilation where the weather is hot.

Install felt-paper window flashing along the bottom and sides of all 4 window openings, then install the windows by nailing the flanges to the framing.

Staple building paper to the wall framing and install the plywood siding. Be careful when handling the sheets of plywood for the upper story.

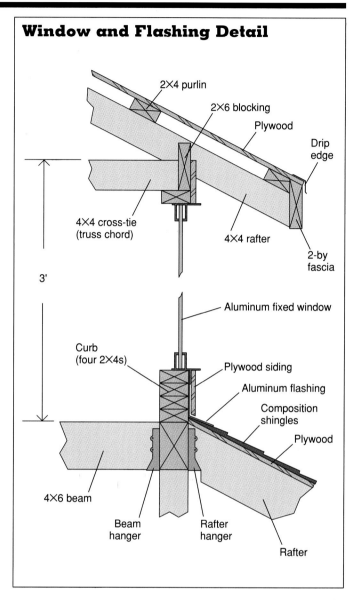

Window and Flashing Detail

2×4 purlin

2×6 blocking

Plywood

Drip edge

4×4 cross-tie (truss chord)

4×4 rafter

2-by fascia

3'

Aluminum fixed window

Curb (four 2×4s)

Plywood siding

Aluminum flashing

Composition shingles

Plywood

4×6 beam

Beam hanger

Rafter hanger

Rafter

Have at least two helpers and avoid this job on a windy day. After the siding is up, install 1×4 trim for the corners and windows. Paint or stain the exterior as you prefer.

Building and Installing the Doors

To build the doors, cut a piece of siding material to size for each door and bolt it to a frame of 1×6s, consisting of vertical members on each side and 3 horizontal rails between them.

Attach the doors to the siding with heavy-duty strap hinges. Secure one of the doors in place with a spring-loaded latch at the top and a cane bolt at the bottom—drill a hole in the header for the latch and a ⅝-inch hole in the concrete floor for the cane bolt. Install another cane bolt at the bottom of the second door, attach a hasp or door latch to the door, and your shed is complete.

JAPANESE-STYLE SHED

This is not a Japanese design per se, but the roofline, cantilevered beams, hip rafters, and shoji-style wall panels suggest a Japanese influence. The structure could be used for storage, or it could be put to a more formal use: the interior space would be appropriate for laying out a buffet and serving guests.

Building the Foundation

This 12-foot-square shed utilizes post-and-beam construction, with 4×4 posts embedded in concrete footings around the perimeter of the structure. These 12-foot-long posts support the floor, walls, and roof.

Begin by digging post-holes at least 3 feet, 4 inches deep. Place about 3 inches of gravel in the bottom of each hole for drainage, then set the posts in place. Make sure that they are plumb, then brace them diagonally with 2×4s. Pour the concrete around the posts; leave the braces in place until the concrete sets.

The foundation plan (see page 58) includes 4 pier blocks in the center of the structure to support the shed floor and 20 pier blocks outside the posts to support the deck. Set the pier blocks into fresh concrete. The tops should be level with one another, at least 8 inches above the ground; use a water level or long straightedge and carpenter's level to place them accurately.

Building the Floor and Deck

After the concrete sets, install the 4×4 beams that support the floor and deck. The 12-foot lengths are for the 2 center beams; the 10-foot lengths are for the 5-foot beams around the perimeter that cantilever beyond the piers; the 8-foot lengths are for the 4-foot fillers that go between the rest of the posts and beams.

Level the beams with shims. Connect the beams to the posts and to one another with 4×4 metal beam hangers. Where 4 beams converge at each post, attach the first 2 beams in one direction with the H-shaped hangers (Simpson HH4 or equivalent); then attach the other 2 beams with the top-flange hangers (Simpson HU44TF or equivalent).

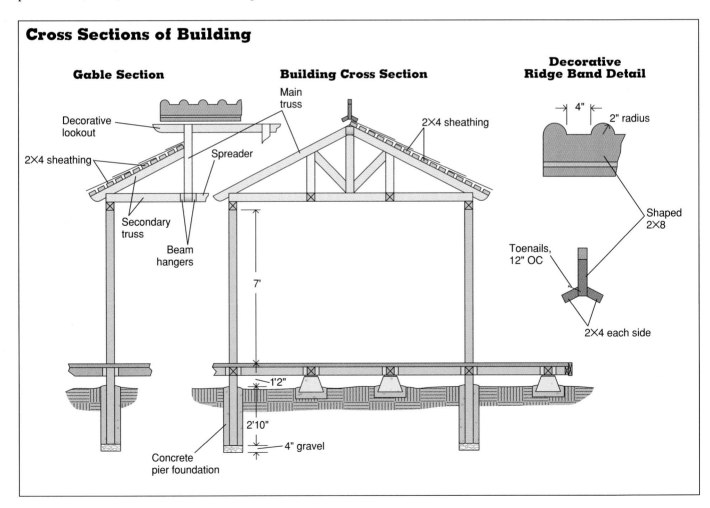

Cross Sections of Building

Gable Section

Building Cross Section

Decorative Ridge Band Detail

Main truss

Decorative lookout

2×4 sheathing

2×4 sheathing

Spreader

Secondary truss

Beam hangers

7'

1'2"

2'10"

4" gravel

Concrete pier foundation

4"

2" radius

Shaped 2×8

Toenails, 12" OC

2×4 each side

Japanese-Style Shed

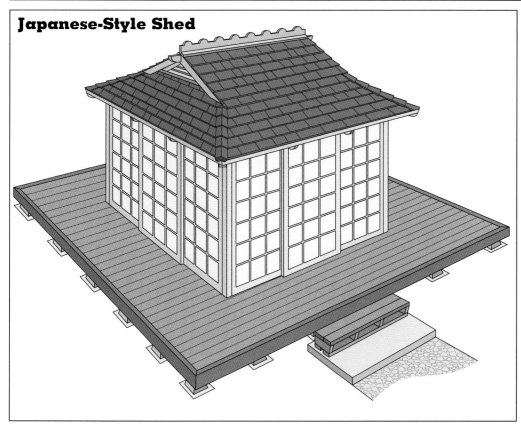

You may have to drill a few holes through the first brackets where they interfere with the nail holes for the second pair of brackets.

When the beams are in place, install the shed floor inside the perimeter posts by blind-nailing 2×6 tongue-and-groove decking boards to the floor beams.

Before installing the exterior decking, install 2×6 trim boards around the perimeter of the deck. Cut 45-degree miter joints for the corners, and fasten the boards with 16d spiral-shank nails so that the top edges are 1½ inches above the tops of the floor beams; predrill at the ends of boards.

Then attach 2×4 cleats to the inside faces of the trim boards to support the ends of the decking boards, screwing them every 12 inches. The tops

Exterior Details

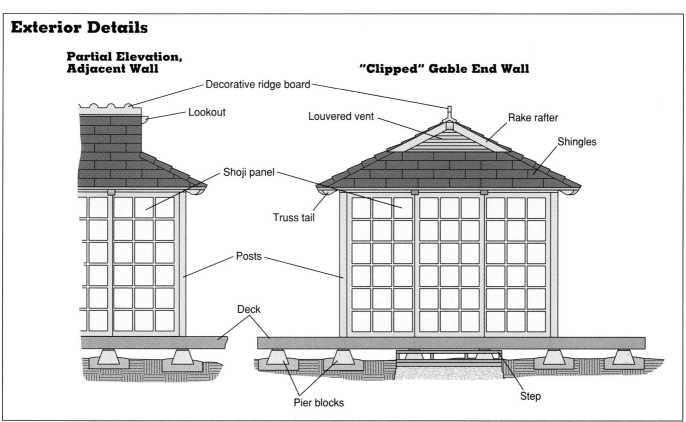

Partial Elevation, Adjacent Wall

"Clipped" Gable End Wall

Decorative ridge board

Lookout

Louvered vent

Rake rafter

Shingles

Shoji panel

Truss tail

Posts

Deck

Pier blocks

Step

Foundation and Framing Plan

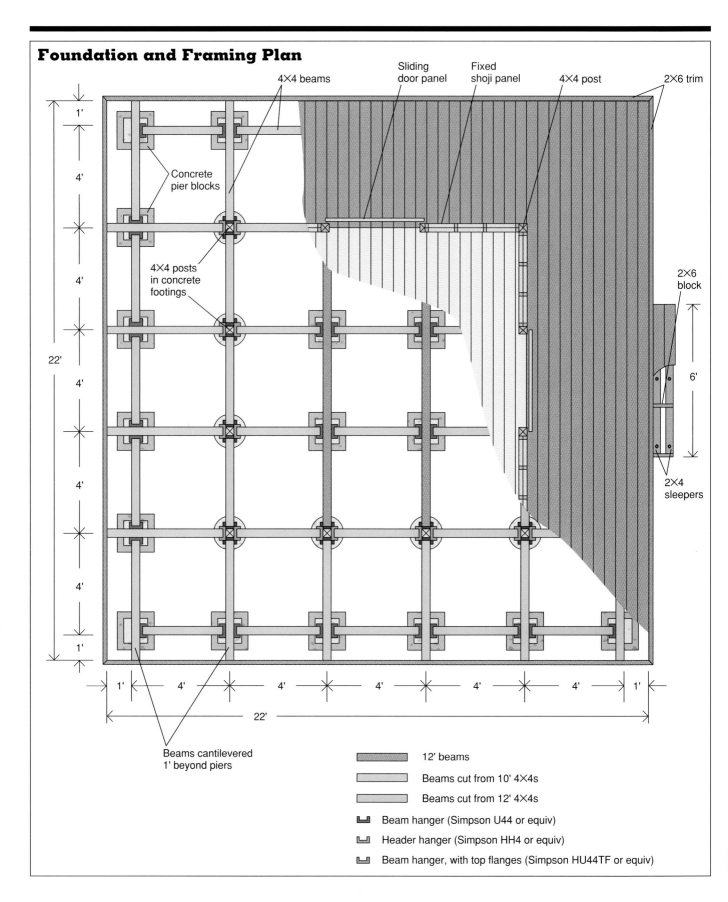

4×4 beams

Sliding door panel

Fixed shoji panel

4×4 post

2×6 trim

Concrete pier blocks

4×4 posts in concrete footings

2×6 block

2×4 sleepers

Beams cantilevered 1' beyond piers

12' beams

Beams cut from 10' 4×4s

Beams cut from 12' 4×4s

Beam hanger (Simpson U44 or equiv)

Header hanger (Simpson HH4 or equiv)

Beam hanger, with top flanges (Simpson HU44TF or equiv)

of the cleats should be 1½ inches below the top edge of the 2×6 trim boards. Finally, cut and lay out the 2×6 decking, then fasten it to the cleats and floor beams with 3-inch by No. 8 deck screws.

Framing the Walls

Frame the walls by trimming all of the posts to exactly 8 feet above the floor and attaching the upper beams to the posts with post-cap hardware.

Framing the Roof

This is not a roof for beginners. It consists of 2 main trusses, 2 secondary trusses, and 4 hip beams, all constructed with 4×4s (see page 60). The roof slope is 6 in 12.

Begin by building the main trusses. First, install the lower chords, or horizontal beams, by attaching them to the support beams with 4×4 end post caps. Prop up the middle of the beams with temporary braces to keep them from sagging until you complete the trusses.

Next, complete the trusses by installing the rafters, king posts, short uprights, and diagonal braces, connecting them with bolts and plywood gussets, as shown (see page 61). Attach beam hangers to each truss for the spreaders and lower members of the secondary trusses, and attach framing anchors for the secondary truss rafters (see page 60). Align them carefully on both sides of the main truss.

Next, hang the 4×4 spreaders between the trusses. Then

cut and install the beams and rafters of the secondary trusses with the same materials and connectors as the main trusses. Attach these to the wall beams and to the framing anchors that you fastened to the main trusses.

Each 4×4 hip rafter requires a compound miter cut—a double miter cut of 45 degrees, compounded by the shorter

hip slope of 6 in 17—to join with the main and secondary trusses. Normally, the bird's mouth for a hip rafter is longer than that on common rafters, which is possible

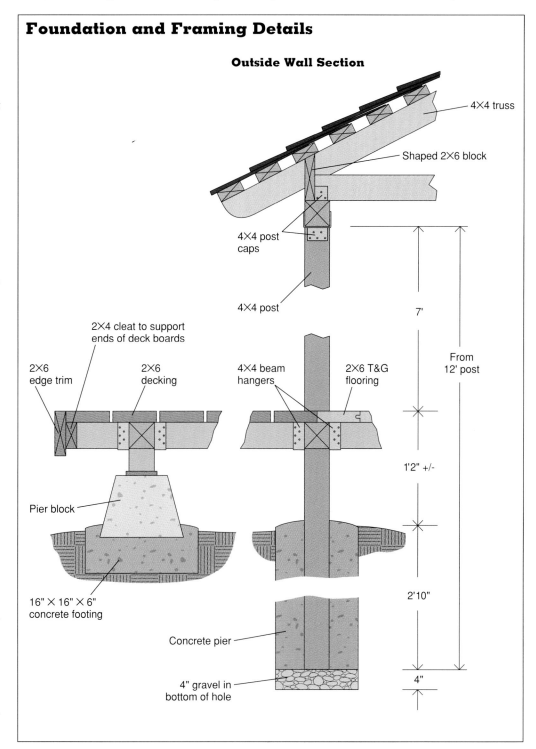

Foundation and Framing Details

Outside Wall Section

4×4 truss

Shaped 2×6 block

4×4 post caps

4×4 post

7'

From 12' post

2×4 cleat to support ends of deck boards

2×6 edge trim

2×6 decking

4×4 beam hangers

2×6 T&G flooring

1'2" +/-

Pier block

16" × 16" × 6" concrete footing

2'10"

Concrete pier

4" gravel in bottom of hole

4"

Roof Plan: Framing and Sheathing

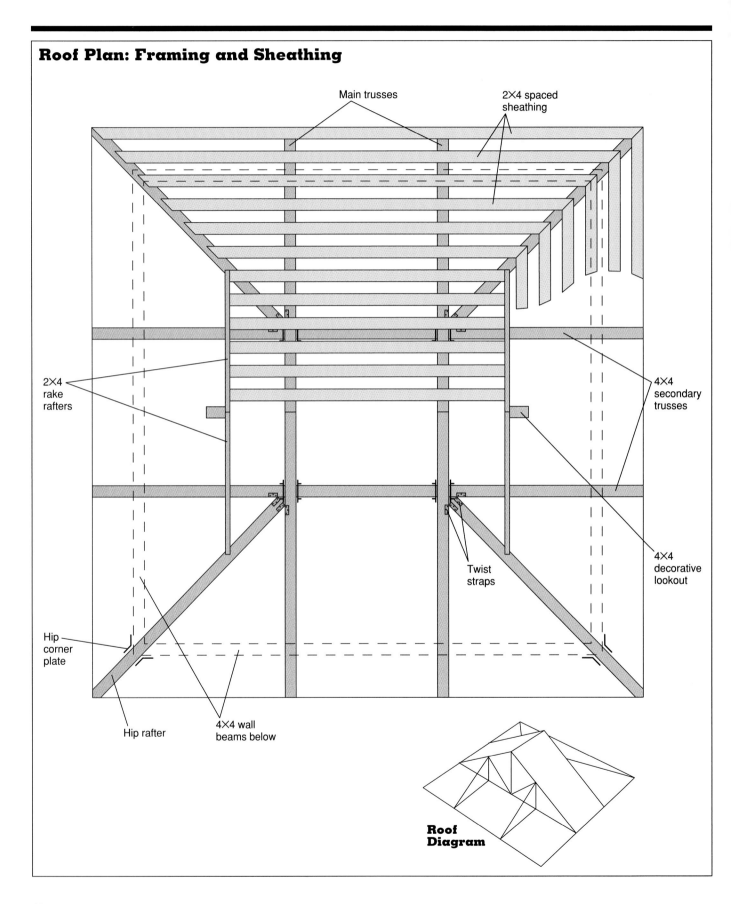

Main trusses

2×4 spaced sheathing

2×4 rake rafters

4×4 secondary trusses

4×4 decorative lookout

Twist straps

Hip corner plate

Hip rafter

4×4 wall beams below

Roof Diagram

Main Truss Diagram

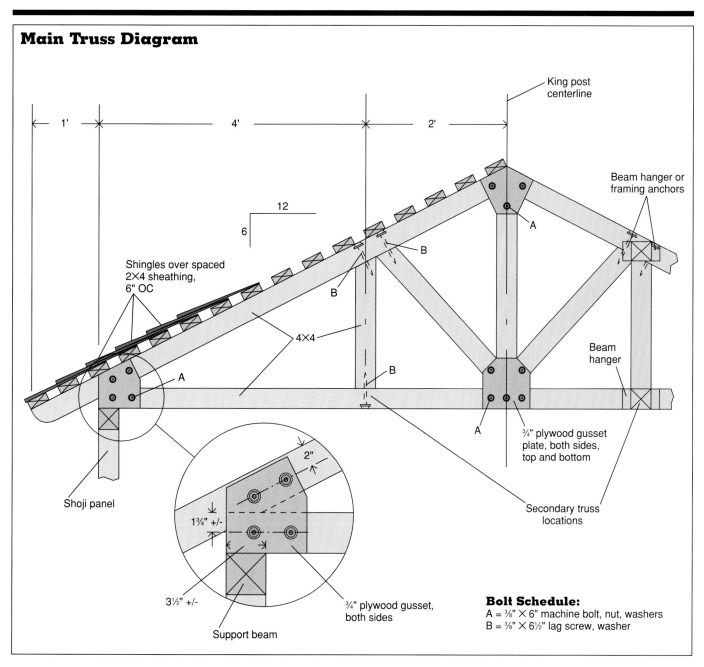

King post centerline

Beam hanger or framing anchors

Shingles over spaced 2×4 sheathing, 6" OC

12

6

4×4

Beam hanger

A

B

B

B

A

A

Shoji panel

2"

1¾" +/-

3½" +/-

Support beam

¾" plywood gusset, both sides

¾" plywood gusset plate, both sides, top and bottom

Secondary truss locations

Bolt Schedule:
A = ⅜" × 6" machine bolt, nut, washers
B = ⅜" × 6½" lag screw, washer

---

because hip rafters are a larger size of lumber. In this design, 4×4s are used for the hips as well as for the common rafters; cut the bird's mouths so that there is 2⅛ inches of rafter left above the deepest part of the cut, measured perpendicularly from the top edge of the rafter. Don't forget the longer overhang, which is shaped at the end.

Lay out and cut the first hip, and check for fit at all 4 locations before you cut the other hip rafters. Install the hip rafters by connecting each to the trusses with 2 twist straps, and to the corners with a hip corner plate.

Sheathing and Shingling the Roof

Before installing the 2×4 sheathing, install the louvered gable vents while access is easy. You can make a large site-built vent for each gable out of 1×4s and window screen (see page 62), or buy standard triangular gable vents and install them in a piece of plywood siding cut to fit the opening. Either way, when you attach the sheathing, use blocking to fill the gaps between the sheathing boards above the vents.

Wood shingles require spaced, not solid, sheathing. Start installing the 2×4 sheathing at the eave and work up the roof slope, spacing the

Roof Details, Side View

Louvered Vent, Gable View

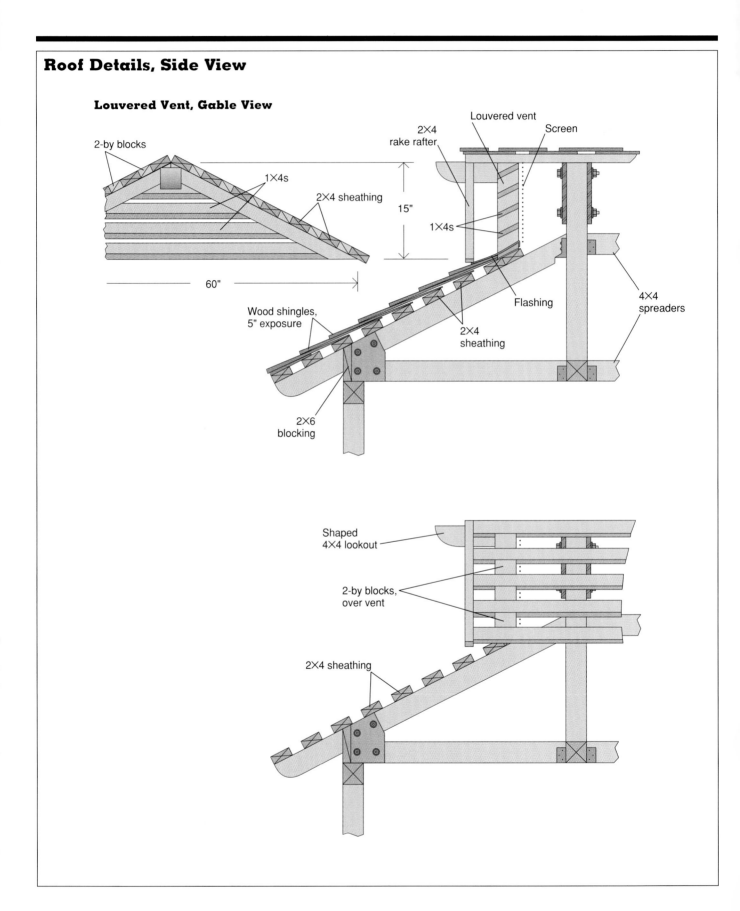

2-by blocks

1×4s

2×4 sheathing

15"

60"

Louvered vent

2×4 rake rafter

Screen

1×4s

Flashing

2×4 sheathing

4×4 spreaders

Wood shingles, 5" exposure

2×6 blocking

Shaped 4×4 lookout

2-by blocks, over vent

2×4 sheathing

boards according to the exposure recommended for the shingles you are using. For instance, for a 5-inch exposure, which is the most common one for wood shingles, the space between the 2×4s should be 1½ inches, so that the 3½-inch-wide boards will be spaced every 5 inches, on center.

After you reach a point 4 feet up the roof, cut the next sheathing boards that cross the main trusses so that they overhang each truss by 16¼ inches, to form the gable overhang. These sheathing boards, and the rest of the sheathing on these 2 sides of the roof, are 84 inches long, with square ends rather than mitered ends.

Complete the sheathing on these 2 sides, then install the sheathing for the other 2 sides under these overhangs. You will have to trim and fit the first few of these boards around the sheathing already in place where the boards intersect the hip rafters.

After installing the sheathing, nail 2×4 rake rafters to the ends of the overhangs. The rake rafters should be pressure-treated wood or redwood. Cut them short at the bottom ends so that there will be enough space to slip the roof shingles under these rafters. Then lag screw a "dummy" 4×4 lookout, shaped the same way as the truss rafter tails, to the rake rafters at each peak.

Install fire-retardant wood shingles over the spaced sheathing, according to the manufacturer's specifications. Nail a strip of angle flashing over the joint where the shingles abut each louvered vent.

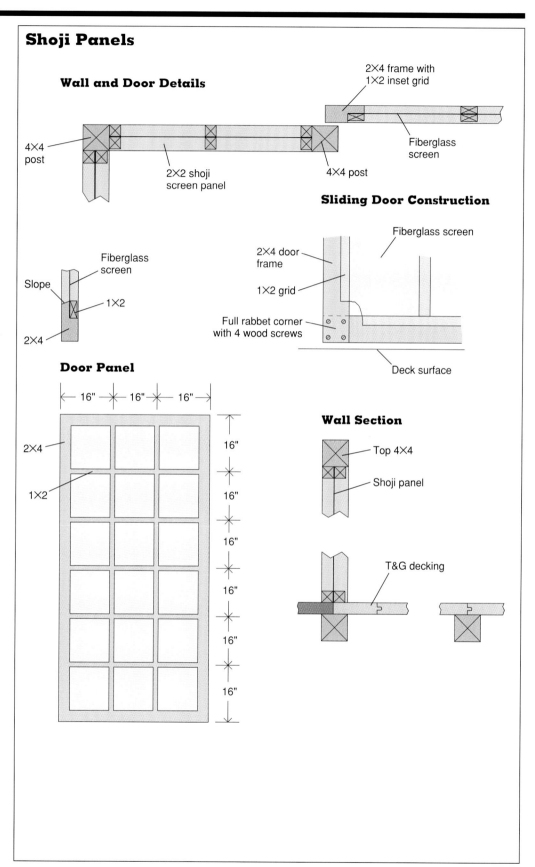

Shoji Panels

Wall and Door Details

2×4 frame with 1×2 inset grid

Fiberglass screen

4×4 post

2×2 shoji screen panel

4×4 post

Fiberglass screen

Slope

1×2

2×4

Sliding Door Construction

Fiberglass screen

2×4 door frame

1×2 grid

Full rabbet corner with 4 wood screws

Deck surface

Door Panel

16"   16"   16"

2×4

1×2

16"

16"

16"

16"

16"

16"

Wall Section

Top 4×4

Shoji panel

T&G decking

Japanese-Style Shed Materials List

Description	Material/Size	Dimension	Qty
Foundation			
Concrete footings			1 cu yd
Pier blocks			24
Concrete			1 cu yd
Gravel			2.5 cu ft
Floor, walls & steps			
Posts	4✕4 PT	12'	12
Beams	4✕4 PT	12'	2
		10'	10
		8'	17
Edge trim	2✕6 PT	14'	4
		10'	4
Cleats & misc	2✕4 PT	12'	4
Flooring	2✕6 T&G pine	12'	26
Decking	2✕6 PT	14'	20
		10'	44
Steps	2✕4 PT	12'	1
	2✕6 PT	8'	2
Top beams	4✕4	12'	4
Shoji frames	2✕2	8'	120
Door frames	2✕4	8'	12
Door mullions & muntins	1✕2	8'	48
Screen material	Fiberglass	4' wide	96 l.f.
Roof			
Main trusses:			
beams	4✕4	12'	2
rafters	4✕4	8'	4
braces	4✕4	12'	2
Spreaders		8'	2
Secondary trusses:			
beams	4✕4	8'	2
rafters	4✕4	12'	2
Hip rafters	4✕4	8'	4
Gussets	¾" AC ply.	4✕8	1
Blocking	2✕6	12'	4
Louvered gable vents	1✕4	10'	4
Sheathing	2✕4	14'	60
Ridge	2✕8	8'	1
Ridge flashing	Sheet metal, 8"	8'	1
Ridge cap	2✕4 cedar	8'	2
	2✕8 cedar	8'	1
Shingles	Fire-retardant wood		536 s.f.

Finish the roof with a 2✕8 decorative ridge board, shaped and cut as shown (see page 56). The scallops on top of the 2✕8 each have a 2-inch radius, and are spaced 8 inches apart, center to center. Toenail it between two 2✕4s, beveled for the 6 in 12 roof slope, with 8d HDG nails. Then set the assembly on the roof ridge and secure it with a 16d HDG nail every 2 feet. Coat the nail heads with roofing caulk.

Making the Wall Panels

The wall panels reflect the distinctive Japanese shoji style. Although the traditional shoji consists of rice paper, this design substitutes thin white fiberglass sheets, which you can cut to fit the panels.

Cut 2✕2s for the mullions (vertical pieces) and muntins (horizontal pieces) of each shoji, measuring the height and width of each wall opening at several places to deter-

Materials List (continued)

Description	Material/Size	Dimension	Qty
Hardware & misc			
Expansion anchors	⅜" bolts	6"	6
4✕4 hangers:			
@ posts	Simpson HH4 or equiv		24
@ posts	Simpson HU44TF or equiv		24
@ beams	Simpson U44 or equiv		44
Post caps	Simpson PC44 or equiv		8
Post caps, corners	Simpson RTC44 or equiv		4
Beam hangers, trusses	Simpson U44 or equiv		12
Framing anchors, trusses	Simpson A35 or equiv		8
Hip corner plates	Simpson CKP4 or equiv		4
Twist straps @ hips	Simpson LTS10 or equiv		8
Lag screws	⅜" ✕ 6½" + washers		16
Lag screws	⅜" ✕ 5"		6
Machine bolts	⅜" ✕ 6" + washers & nuts		50
Nails & screws	As needed		
Roofing caulk	Tube		1
Silicone caulk	Tube		4
Window screen, or 14" louvered vents		3' width	5'
Sliding door track & guide		8'	4

mine exact lengths (see page 63). Mark the 2×2s where they will intersect each other, so that you can cut notches for interlocking lap joints.

Position the mullions and muntins so that the vertical mullions appear continuous and the horizontal muntins fit between them. Assemble the frames with glue and 6d finishing nails. The frames are identical for each side.

Once you have assembled all the frames, cut the fiberglass to size, allowing approximately ⅛ inch all around for expansion.

To complete each shoji, first install the exterior frame in the wall opening. Apply a bead of silicone caulk under the bottom muntin, or sill, and nail the frame in place with 16d galvanized finishing nails; the outside face should be set in ¼ inch from the outside edges of the posts.

Squeeze a continuous bead of caulk on the back of the exterior frame members and press the fiberglass panel gently into place against the frame, allowing the silicone to spread. Don't worry if some silicone oozes beyond the frame; you can wait until it sets and trim it with a dull putty knife.

The silicone will hold the fiberglass in place while you install the interior frame assembly. Do not caulk it. Install the rest of the panels the same way.

Step Detail

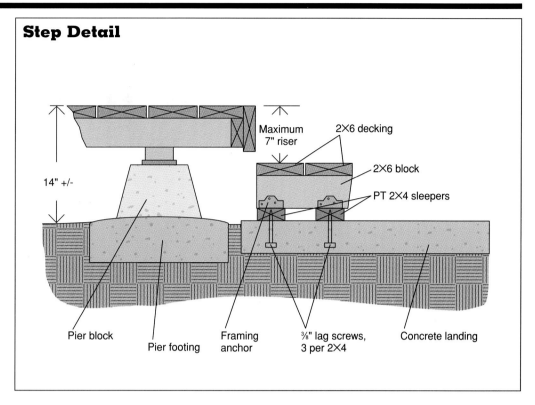

14" +/-

Maximum 7" riser

2×6 decking

2×6 block

PT 2×4 sleepers

Pier block

Pier footing

Framing anchor

⅜" lag screws, 3 per 2×4

Concrete landing

Making the Sliding Doors

Prepare for the sliding doors by installing lower guides on the floor and upper roller guides on the lower edges of the beams. The upper guides will function the same as they do for sliding closet doors.

For the door frames, use 2×4s for the stiles (vertical members) and rails (horizontal members). Rabbet the ends of each 2×4 for half-lap joints. Cut ⅞-inch by ⅜-inch rabbets into the interior edges of the stiles and rails. Drill pilot holes for 1¼-inch by No. 8 deck screws; glue and screw the stiles and rails together, then set the door frame aside.

While the glue dries, cut 1×2s for the mullions and muntins. The pieces for the interior side should be ¾ inch longer than those for the exterior, to account for the rabbets.

As you did with the shoji panels, assemble the doors so that the mullions appear continuous. Apply glue to the ends of the mullions and muntins of the exterior assembly, set it into the door frame, and toenail the mullions and muntins to the frame with 4d HDG finishing nails. Apply caulk to the frame, insert the fiberglass panel, apply caulk to the fiberglass, and press the interior grid into place. Nail the grid to the door frame with 6d HDG finishing nails.

To hang the doors, attach roller hardware, the type used for closed bypass doors, to the top of each door and hang them from the upper door track. You can adjust the height of the doors by turning adjusting screws in the roller brackets.

Making the Steps

Construct a step on a concrete landing. After pouring and smoothing the concrete, set two 6-foot-long pressure-treated 2×4 sleepers, with ⅜-inch by 5-inch lag screws in the bottoms, on the wet concrete, as shown (see above).

Then cut four 12-inch-long 2×6 blocks to set on the sleepers. Rip the blocks so that, when set on edge, they will elevate the step to create 2 intervals of equal height. Attach the blocks to the sleepers with framing anchors.

For the step, set two 2×6s over the blocks. Now the building is ready for whatever painting or decorative detailing you prefer.

GAZEBO OFFICE/STORAGE

A gazebo offers a variation on the usual recti-linear shapes—and interesting building challenges as well. Most gazebos are intended as outdoor retreats, but this one is enclosed to provide a home office and storage space. It might also be used as an art studio or a potting shed.

Office and Storage

Whether managing a family, running a business, or working at home, many people are finding it more and more desirable to have an office at home. They need space to work and house their office equipment, filing cabinets, papers, and other business paraphernalia. This gazebo provides a unique, private place with ample work space, plenty of light, and built-in storage.

The possibilities for finishing this "shed" are limitless. If

Gazebo Office/Storage

Gazebo Materials List

Description	Material/Size	Dimension	Qty
Foundation			
Gravel			1.4 cu yd
Concrete			2.8 cu yd
Rebar	#4	20'	As required
Wire mesh	6X6/10,10	12' X 12'	144 s.f.
Sand			0.7 cu yd
Dobie blocks	As needed		
Wall framing			
Posts & hub	6X6	8'	7
		10'	1
Top plates	4X6	10'	4
Sill plates	2X6 PT	10'	4
Misc framing	2X6	8'	17
Door header	4X6	4'	1
Roof			
Rafters	2X6	10'	8
Blocking	2X4	10'	4
Decking	2X6 T&G		192 s.f.
Insulation	1"–2" rigid foam		192 s.f.
Fascia	2X8	12'	4
Sheathing	½" CDX ply.	4X8	6
Underlayment	15-lb felt		192 s.f.
Drip edge	Galvanized	12'	8
Shingles	Composition		192 s.f.
Hip shingles	Hip & ridge or equiv		72 l.f.
Flashing	Metal (must be fabricated)		
Exterior finish			
Panel plywood	½" ACX ply.	4X8	9–15
Panel insulation	1" rigid foam	4X8	4–6
Panel stops	1X1	8'	24
Panel caps	2X6	10'	4
Windows	Single hung	4'0" X 5'0"	3–7
Door	Divided lites	3'0" X 6'8"	1
Window casing	1X6		Varies
Top plate trim	1X6	10'	4
Post trim	1X6	8'	16
Sill trim	1X3	10'	4
Paint/stain	Varies		Varies
Interior finish			
Wall covering	Varies		Varies
Trim	Varies		Varies
Flooring	Sheet vinyl, 12' width		12 l.f.
Fixtures, built-ins	Varies		Varies
Paint	Varies		1 gal.

Gazebo Floor Plan

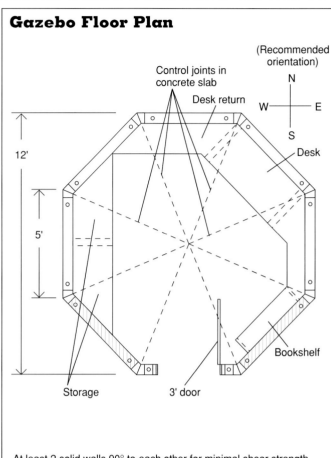

At least 2 solid walls 90° to each other for minimal shear strength

West-facing walls can be solid instead of glazed, to act as glare block for low-angle sun from west

Materials List (continued)

Description	Material/Size	Dimension	Qty
Hardware & misc			
Anchor bolts	½" dia	3"	16
Column bases	6X6 (Simpson CB66 or equiv)		8
Angle clips	Simpson A34 or equiv		32
Straps @ corners	1½" X 12"		8
Plumber's strap	Steel	40' roll	2
Lag screws		½" X 12"	16
Machine bolts with nuts		⅜" X 6"	32
Nails & screws	As needed		
Caulk	Exterior, tube		8
Window flashing	Paper, roll	6"	Varies

you prefer a wilderness out-post, simply build the basic structure and finish it with window screens, a few electrical outlets, and a light stain. At the other end of the spectrum, you may want to make your office as luxurious as you can, with fine residential wood windows, a full wood door of corresponding quality, built-up interior trim, finished wall paneling, carpet, heavy wall and ceiling insulation, built-in storage units, a full

lighting system, heating, and telecommunications hookups.

The design also gives you options for finishing the walls with solid panels or windows. For structural rigidity, at least 2 walls that are 90 degrees to each other should be solid panels. For most locations, 3 solid walls and 5 window walls provide a nice balance between natural light and wall space, but you can adapt this design to suit your site and working requirements.

Consider all of these options early in your planning, because they may affect some of the construction techniques. For example, the post-and-panel system of construction makes it difficult to run wiring after the gazebo is built. Plan your outlets and lighting scheme before starting construction, so that you can place conduits in the concrete slab to make wiring easier.

Also, if you choose certain wood windows, they will

require larger rough openings than the window size specified in this design. Consult the manufacturer's specifications; some may require 2 inches more width and more than an additional 2 inches of height.

Finally, consider an option for the slab that is decorative and practical: control joints radiating out from the center of the floor to the 8 corners, to minimize cracking and create visual interest.

Section/Interior Elevation

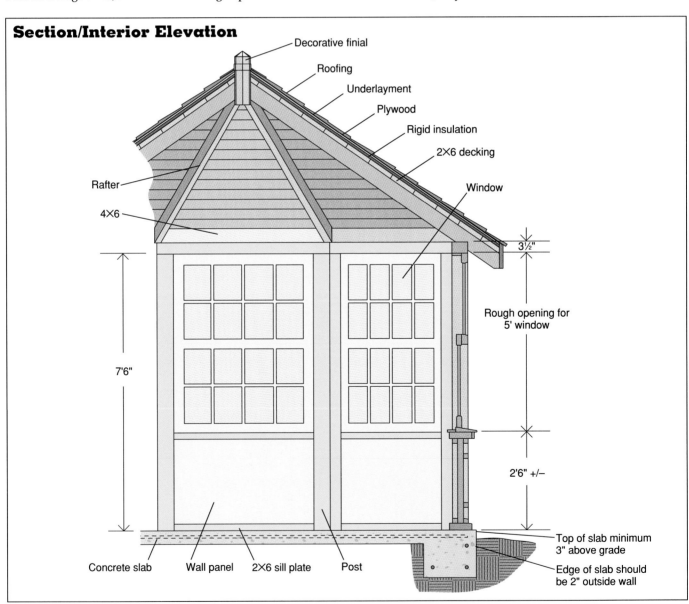

Decorative finial
Roofing
Underlayment
Plywood
Rigid insulation
2×6 decking
Window
Rafter
4×6
3½"
Rough opening for 5' window
7'6"
2'6" +/−
Top of slab minimum 3" above grade
Edge of slab should be 2" outside wall
Concrete slab   Wall panel   2×6 sill plate   Post

Building the Foundation

The foundation for this gazebo is an octagonal slab, 2 inches wider than the building all around, with enlarged footings at the corners (see right).

After leveling the site, lay out the octagon by building batter boards and laying string lines for a 12-foot square (see right). Measure the diagonals to verify the square.

Establish the corners of a second square, rotated 45 degrees from the first square. The intersections of the squares are the points of the gazebo.

Next, using the layout strings for reference, stake 2×8 form boards 2 inches beyond the building perimeter for the slab. Dig a 12-inch-wide footing trench just inside the form boards, to the depth required by local code. At the corners, extend the trench under the form boards, as shown (see right), to provide an 18-inch-square footing area under each post.

Excavate 4 inches of soil from the slab area and bury any pipes or conduits required for under-slab runs. Spread 4 inches of gravel and 2 inches of sand for the slab base, install a plastic vapor barrier over the sand, and cover it with an additional 2 inches of sand. Place horizontal ½-inch rebar in the footing trenches and reinforcing mesh over the entire area. Wrap pipes and conduits with insulation where they will be surrounded by concrete.

Before pouring the concrete, be sure you know exactly where and how you will set

Layout for Foundation

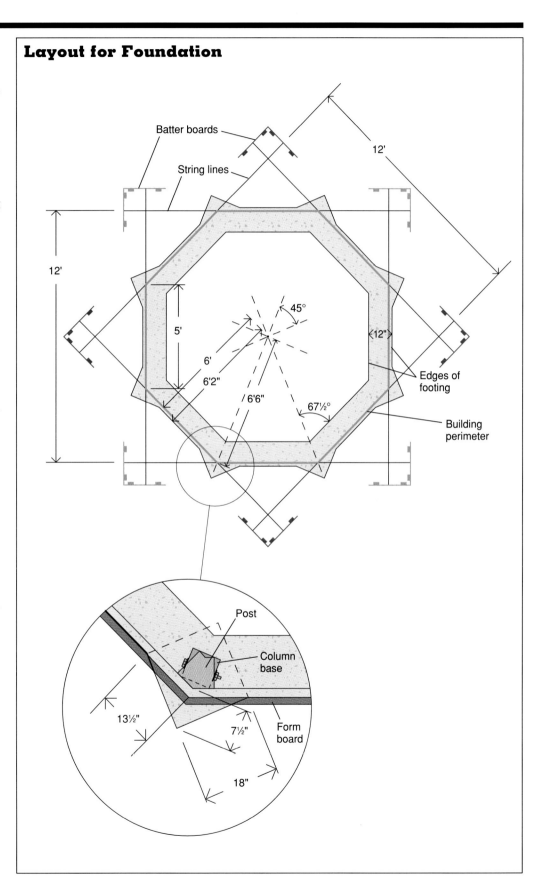

Post and Corner Details

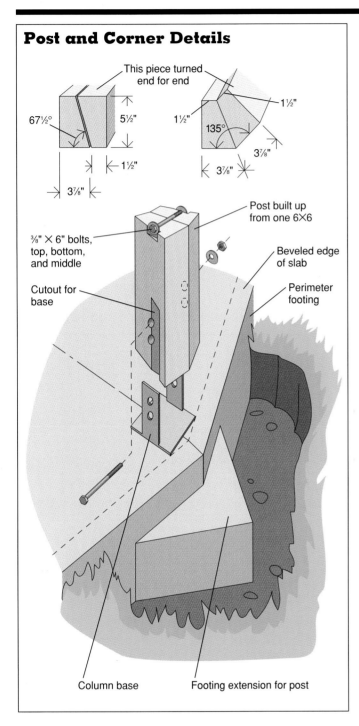

This piece turned end for end

$67\frac{1}{2}°$ $5\frac{1}{2}$" $1\frac{1}{2}$" $135°$ $1\frac{1}{2}$" $3\frac{7}{8}$" $1\frac{1}{2}$" $3\frac{7}{8}$" $3\frac{7}{8}$" $3\frac{7}{8}$"

$\frac{3}{8}$" × 6" bolts, top, bottom, and middle

Post built up from one 6×6

Cutout for base

Beveled edge of slab

Perimeter footing

Column base

Footing extension for post

the column bases, or post anchors, for the 6×6 posts (see above). The built-up posts won't fit squarely in the column bases—you will have to shave the sides of the posts— but everything will line up perfectly if you simply place

each column base so that the 5½-inch-square plate is centered over the radial axis of the octagon, and the outside corners of the plate barely touch the perimeter of the building line.

Pour the concrete, embed the column bases, and place a 3-inch anchor bolt within 12 inches of each side for the sill plates, except where the door will go. Set anchor bolts in that opening for a short sill plate on one side of the door. Finish the slab surface as desired. Create control joints in a pleasing pattern, such as 4 or 8 spokes radiating from the center, or a tic-tac-toe grid aligned with the octagon corners.

Building and Installing the Posts

Fabricate 8 posts from 8-foot 6×6s by slicing them in two and bolting the pieces together into a new shape (see left). To cut the posts lengthwise, set your circular saw blade for a 67½-degree bevel cut and cut from both sides of the 6×6, end to end. Practice on a scrap of 6×6 to fine-tune the dimensions; different saw blades cut different kerfs.

You can build the posts ahead of time—it's a good project for winter, before the building season—or while the concrete is setting. To install each post, cut notches to let in the brackets of the column base; hold the post in place to mark for the cuts. After cutting, set the post in place, brace it, drill a hole for the lower bolt, and install the bolt. (Don't drill holes and install the top bolts until after all the posts are in place and the 4×6 top plates are installed.) Don't worry about the protruding column base bracket and bolt heads; they will be covered by 2×6s; however, shield sharp edges during construction.

Installing the Top Plates

Cut 4×6 top plates with 22½-degree angles at the ends. Fasten the plates to the posts with metal angle brackets and/or ½-inch by 12-inch lag screws. Fasten 12-inch-long straps on top of the plates to tie them together.

Install the plates, then fasten plumber's strap all the way around the outside edges of the plates with 16d HDG nails, every 12 inches. This will prevent the structure from spreading. Don't worry about the strap's appearance; your finish trim will hide it completely.

Building the Roof

Before you cut the rafters, cut an octagonal center hub from a 6×6 (see page 72). It should be 16 to 24 inches long, depending on how you decorate the top—by detailing the top portion of the hub or by adding a manufactured finial.

Next, cut a pair of 2×6 rafters for an 8 in 12 roof slope (see page 71 bottom). Cut the rafters as if they were common rafters for an 8 in 12 slope; note, however, if you are used to working with rafter tables, that these are neither common rafters nor true hip rafters for a 12-foot-wide structure. The 8 in 12 roof measurement is for cutting the rafters only; the roof itself, as measured on the roof planes, is slightly steeper (8.444 in 12). Test these first 2 rafters for fit before cutting the other six.

Installing the rafters requires 2 people. First, fasten

Attaching Top Plates

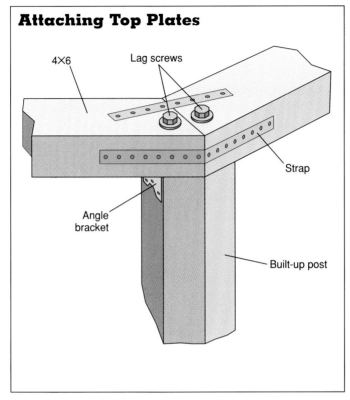

4×6

Lag screws

Strap

Angle bracket

Built-up post

angle clips to the top plates at the corners, 1½ inches apart. Then lay planks across the top plates for scaffolding and make a temporary support for the hub.

Begin assembly by attaching the tops of the test rafters to opposite sides of the hub with 4-inch by No. 8 deck screws (predrill to prevent splitting). Tip up this assembly, slide the temporary support under the hub, and tack the rafters to the clips at the bird's mouths. Check to be sure that the hub is centered over the building.

You will notice that the bottoms of the rafters are not flush with the inside edges of the top plates, because the bird's-mouth drop cuts are only 2 inches—the maximum

cut to preserve the strength of the overhangs. If you prefer the rafter bottoms to be flush with the top plates for visual purposes, use 2×8 rafter stock and cut the bird's mouths 3¾ inches deep.

After checking the rafters for fit, remove the assembly, make any adjustments, and cut the rest of the rafters. Reassemble the first two, then attach 2 more rafters perpendicular to them.

Once the first 4 rafters are in place, the rest are easy. Install them one at a time. Then, cut frieze blocks to fit between the rafters; the ends should have 22½-degree bevels. Toenail these to the plates and facenail into them through the rafters with 16d HDG nails.

Rafter Details

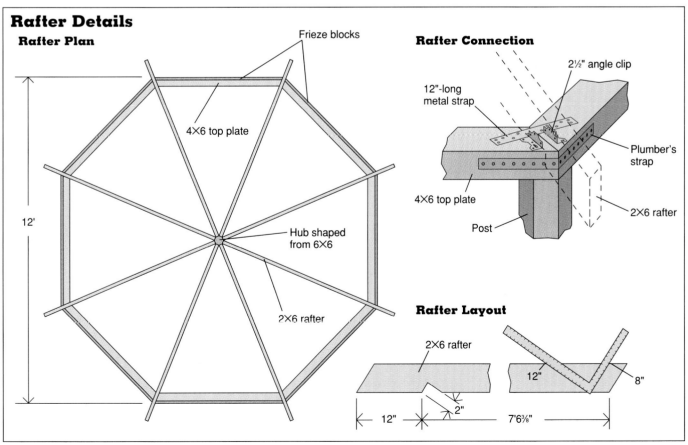

Rafter Plan

Frieze blocks

4×6 top plate

12'

Hub shaped from 6×6

2×6 rafter

Rafter Connection

2½" angle clip

12"-long metal strap

4×6 top plate

Post

Plumber's strap

2×6 rafter

Rafter Layout

2×6 rafter

12"

8"

12"

2"

7'6⅜"

Hub Detail

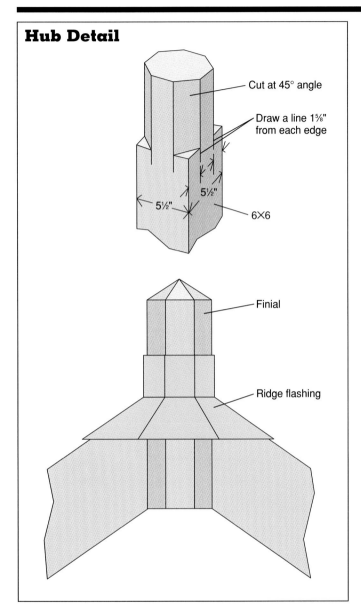

Cut at 45° angle

Draw a line 1⅝" from each edge

5½"

5½"

6×6

Finial

Ridge flashing

Lower Wall Panel Detail

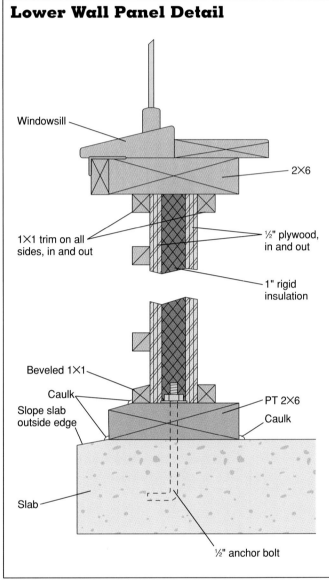

Windowsill

2×6

1×1 trim on all sides, in and out

½" plywood, in and out

1" rigid insulation

Beveled 1×1

Caulk

PT 2×6

Slope slab outside edge

Caulk

Slab

½" anchor bolt

Now install the roof decking. Cut one end of each 2×6 with a compound cut: a miter cut of 19 degrees (4⅛ and 12 on the framing square) on the face, with the saw blade set for a 15-degree bevel. With this end positioned over the center of a rafter, nail the board in place.

After installing 3 or 4 boards the same way, carefully set your saw depth, with a 15-degree bevel, and trim the overhanging ends of the boards. Repeat this process until you get to the final bay, where you will have to cut boards to length before nailing them down. As you approach the top, the pieces become shorter. Predrill these to prevent splitting.

Cut rigid foam insulation to fit over the top of the roof decking and fasten it with screws. Nail fascia boards to the ends of the rafters; they should cover the edges of the insulation. Cut plywood

sheathing into large triangles to fit over the insulation, with bevels along the edges. Nail it through the insulation into the decking, 8 inches on center along the edges. Use 8d box nails for 1-inch-thick insulation, 16d box nails for 2-inch-thick insulation.

Next, install the drip edge, apply roofing underlayment, and cover that with composition shingles according to the manufacturer's instructions. Cover each hip with hip-and-

ridge shingles, or cut individual shingles from the 3-tab shingles.

Enclosing the Gazebo

Install pressure-treated 2×6 sill plates between the posts. Cut each sill plate to fit, then mark and drill holes for the anchor bolts. Apply 2 continuous beads of caulk along the bottom of each sill plate, turn the sill plate over and set it in place, and attach the washers and nuts to the anchor bolts.

Frame the sides of the openings with 2×6s screwed to the posts with 3-inch by No. 8 deck screws. Cut notches or slots in the bottoms of the 2×6s to clear the column bases, and drill shallow holes to clear any protruding bolt heads.

Install a lower wall panel in each opening except where the door will go. These panels consist of 1-inch-thick rigid insulation sandwiched between two ½-inch plywood panels. Make the lower wall panels 2 feet, 6 inches high and 4 feet, 1 inch wide (verify measurements).

For a decorative touch, glue and nail strips of molding into a simple rectangle on the outside face of each panel. To install a panel, nail the exterior 1×1 stops to the sill plate and side framing; bevel the bottom stop, and apply a bead of caulk to each stop before nailing it in place with 6d HDG box nails. Apply another bead of caulk to the inside faces of the stops and set the insulated plywood panel in place. Secure it with stops on the interior side. Then nail stops to the bottom side of the 2×6 panel cap, place the assembly on top of the panels, and screw it to the framing with deck screws.

Once the panels are in, you're ready to install the 4-foot by 5-foot single-hung windows, following the manufacturer's instructions. Before installing the windows, apply paper window flashing around each opening, then caulk the back side of the nailing flanges.

For walls without windows, build insulated panels to fit into the window openings. Install them the same way as the lower panels but without the 2×6 cap.

This design calls for a 3-foot-wide prehung door. Frame a door opening between two of the posts. Use 2×6s, or 2×4s with 1-by jambs, depending on how you will finish the interior walls.

To finish the exterior, nail 1-by trim or decorative molding over all exposed joints and framing members. Back-prime the trim pieces, and use caulk behind any horizontal pieces near the ground. Stain or paint the gazebo as soon as possible to protect the wood.

Finishing the Interior

The interior walls and trim can be finished according to the style you prefer. You can use wood paneling or wallboard for the wall surfaces. For trim, use 1-inch clear lumber or standard moldings, such as casings and baseboards.

Although there is relatively little wall surface in this building, finishing the interior walls will be time consuming because of the angles. Plan to spend several enjoyable days or evenings.

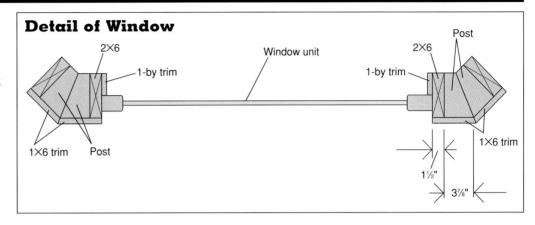

Detail of Window

2×6 · 1-by trim · Window unit · 2×6 · Post · 1-by trim · 1×6 trim · Post · 1×6 trim · 1½" · 3⅞"

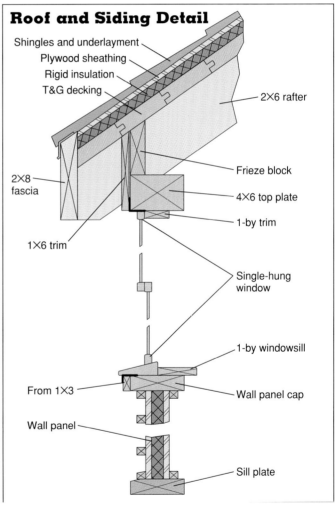

Roof and Siding Detail

Shingles and underlayment · Plywood sheathing · Rigid insulation · T&G decking · 2×6 rafter · Frieze block · 4×6 top plate · 1-by trim · 2×8 fascia · 1×6 trim · Single-hung window · 1-by windowsill · From 1×3 · Wall panel cap · Wall panel · Sill plate

After painting or staining the office, installing the electrical fixtures, and laying the flooring, you can configure your work space. There are storage cabinets under a counter to the left of the door.

On the right is a desk, and bookshelves sit beyond. These can be modular units, custom built-ins, or free-standing furniture pieces.

ENGLISH COTTAGE

This shed is a charmer. Incorporating work space and storage space, it is suitable for many purposes—it could be an office, playhouse, a workroom, or a storeroom. The rich detail makes it fairly complex to build; you may want to hire a professional carpenter. Refer to the Basic Gable-Roofed Shed (page 25) for basic building techniques.

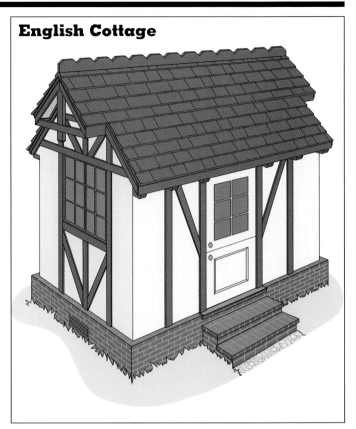

English Cottage

Construction

This shed is in the style of an English Tudor cottage. The structural framing is virtually identical to that of the 8-foot by 12-foot Basic Gable-Roofed Shed (see page 25), but the finish details are significantly different. Cement plaster exterior walls, wallboard and texture in the interior, decorative brick, and ornamental out-board gable truss details require significantly more work. The Dutch door and double casement window lend a traditional touch.

Building the Foundation

Begin with a perimeter foundation (see page 24). Level the site. Dig a trench 12 inches

Elevations

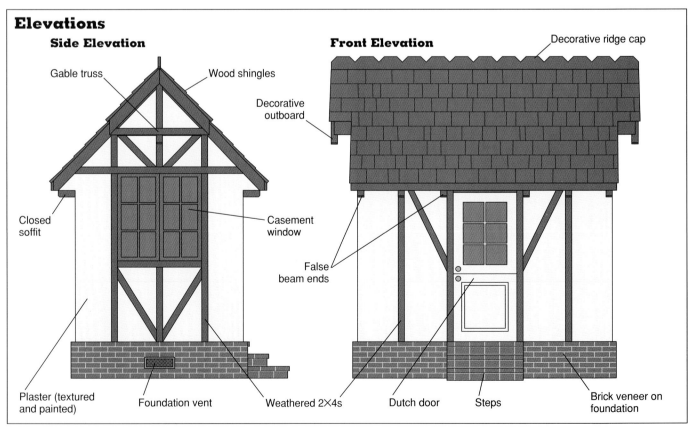

Side Elevation

Gable truss

Wood shingles

Closed soffit

Casement window

Plaster (textured and painted)

Foundation vent

Weathered 2×4s

Front Elevation

Decorative ridge cap

Decorative outboard

False beam ends

Dutch door

Steps

Brick veneer on foundation

deep and 12 inches wide for a continuous footing to set blocks on. If you prefer a poured concrete wall to blocks, build forms that extend at least 18 inches above grade. In either case, the top of the footing should be flush with the grade, at least on the exterior side, to form a foundation for the brick veneer. Remember to form a pad for the steps at the door, including a landing below the bottom step.

In the bottom of the footing trench set 2 courses of No. 4 (½ inch) rebar on 3-inch dobies. Pour the concrete, vibrate, and screed it. After it sets, lay 3 courses of 8-inch by 16-inch concrete blocks. Omit one block in each wall for a vent hole. Do not apply the decorative brick at this time.

Building the Floor, Walls, and Roof

Use pressure-treated joists for the floor framing, as added protection against moisture migrating through the brick veneer (there will also be metal flashing between the joists and brick).

Construct a standard subfloor with tongue-and-groove AC or PTS (plugged-and-touch-sanded) plywood. Before you nail the plywood, cut out a 2-foot by 3-foot opening at either end and construct a small frame between the joists to create an access panel.

For the walls, use standard 2×4 framing with studs 16 inches on center. This shed has a door on one side and 3 windows, but you can frame for

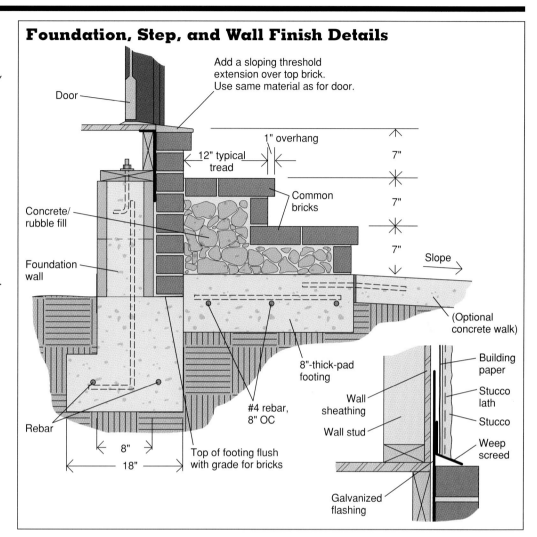

Foundation, Step, and Wall Finish Details

Door

Add a sloping threshold extension over top brick. Use same material as for door.

1" overhang

12" typical tread

7"

Common bricks

Concrete/rubble fill

7"

Foundation wall

7"

Slope

(Optional concrete walk)

8"-thick-pad footing

Building paper

Wall sheathing

Stucco lath

Wall stud

Stucco

Rebar

#4 rebar, 8" OC

Weep screed

8"

18"

Top of footing flush with grade for bricks

Galvanized flashing

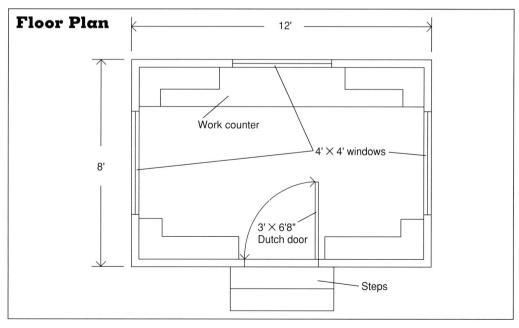

Floor Plan

12'

Work counter

4' × 4' windows

8'

3' × 6'8" Dutch door

Steps

Roof Plan

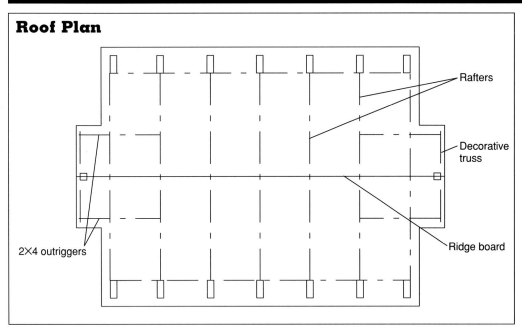

Rafters

Decorative truss

Ridge board

2×4 outriggers

Foundation and Floor Frame

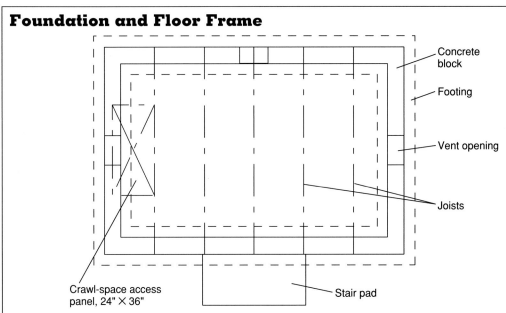

Concrete block

Footing

Vent opening

Joists

Crawl-space access panel, 24" × 36"

Stair pad

these openings in other locations if you prefer.

The decorative gable has a 1-foot overhang at the peak, but the rest of the roof at the rakes terminates just beyond the wall. When you frame the roof, cut rafters for a 12 in 12 slope with a single collar tie for each rafter. Cut the ridge to 14 feet.

You need 4 outriggers at each end to support the decorative trusses. Notch the outriggers into the end rafters and butt and nail them to the inboard rafters.

When you cut the roof sheathing, let it overhang the rafters 3½ inches to account for the exterior plywood, cement plaster, decorative rake board,

and trim (see page 79). Don't complete the decorative truss until after you have applied the cement plaster on the walls, but install the fascia boards.

Next, nail down ½-inch CDX plywood roof sheathing, with the C side down. Follow this with 2 layers of 30-pound felt underlayment and wood shakes, applied according to

the manufacturer's instructions. When you reach the ridge, apply a decorative ridge cap.

Building the Exterior Walls

Install ⅜-inch CDX plywood sheathing on the walls. Nail 2×2 nailers at the top for the soffit (see opposite) and nail ½-inch plywood to the nailers and rafters for the soffit.

Next, you will install the windows. They should have factory-installed stucco trim. Then, staple 2 layers of building paper over the plywood on the entire wall. To simulate old timbers, nail weathered 2×4s to the studs with 16d HDG nails. To simulate beam ends, install short 4×4s under the soffits every 24 inches. Use deck screws, driven at an angle.

Now install the window into the opening. Install louvered gable vents or soffit vents, as needed.

Attach a 12-inch-wide band of galvanized flashing around the bottom of the wall so that it covers the rim joist and foundation sill. Nail galvanized metal weep screeds over this flashing, at floor level, along the bottom of the wall.

Now affix stucco wire with furring nails, or self-furring wire plaster lath, over the building paper to manufacturer specifications. Reinforce the lath at the corners with wire corner moldings.

Follow carefully the manufacturer's instructions on the cement bag when you mix the cement plaster, which is also called stucco. It needs to be the correct consistency to adhere properly. Cement plaster requires at least 2 coats.

Roof Details

Eave Detail at Door

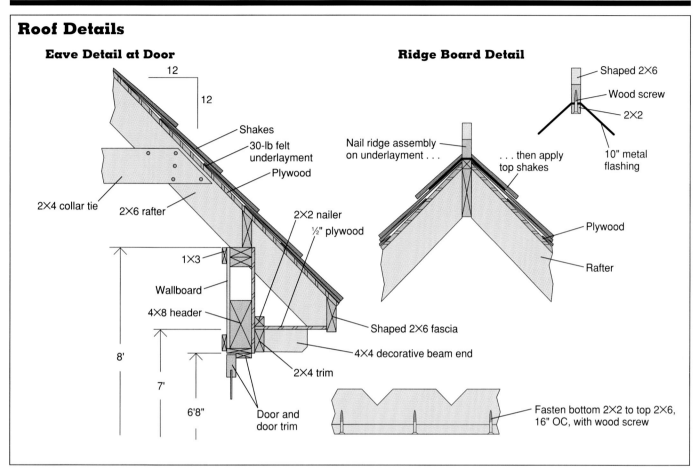

12
12

Shakes
30-lb felt underlayment
Plywood

2×4 collar tie
2×6 rafter
2×2 nailer
½" plywood

1×3
Wallboard
4×8 header

8'
7'
6'8"

Door and door trim

2×4 trim
4×4 decorative beam end
Shaped 2×6 fascia

Ridge Board Detail

Shaped 2×6
Wood screw
2×2

Nail ridge assembly on underlayment . . .
. . . then apply top shakes
10" metal flashing

Plywood
Rafter

Fasten bottom 2×2 to top 2×6, 16" OC, with wood screw

Layers of a Cement Plaster (Stucco) Wall

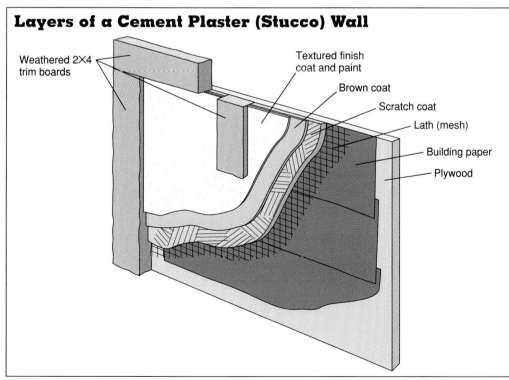

Weathered 2×4 trim boards

Textured finish coat and paint
Brown coat
Scratch coat
Lath (mesh)
Building paper
Plywood

Trowel on the first coat, or "scratch coat," so it covers the wire lath—about ½ to ⅝ inch thick. After it stiffens but before it sets, drag a stucco rake over it to create scratches, which will ensure better adherence for the next coat. Let the scratch coat dry for a few days.

Next, trowel on the "brown coat" or "smooth coat." Again, manufacturer's recommendations are key, because cement needs to cure at the appropriate rate in order to avoid cracking, weakness, and leakage.

Finishing cement plaster can be fun. There are dozens of surface textures that you can achieve by hand, such as swirl and exaggerated trowel marks. Follow mixing directions and texture the surface to your taste. Traditionally, this kind of surface looks rustic, so the rougher you make it, the more authentic it will be.

Many finish coats already contain specific colors, so painting is optional. You can simulate old English white-wash with latex paint; it acts as a water-repellent layer. This is particularly important when you consider that cement natu-rally absorbs water. In freezing climates, the less water that seeps into the plaster, the longer it will last. Before apply-ing the finish coat, be sure to use the appropriate primer for cement surfaces.

Building the Gable Trusses

After you complete the cement plaster and paint, nail the 2×6 rake rafters to the ends of the outriggers at both gables. Also toenail through the face into the ridge. Now you can attach the decorative collar tie to the outriggers, with a decorative post attaching to the ridge.

Applying Foundation Brick

The time to apply the decora-tive brick is after you have finished plastering and paint-ing. This avoids the inevitable spattering of cement and paint (although you may prefer some spattering for effect). Used bricks are best—although not absolutely nec-essary—for a rustic appear-ance. Mix the mortar accord-ing to the recommendations on the bag.

English Cottage Materials List

Description	Material/Size	Dimension	Qty
Foundation			
Concrete	For 12"-deep footing		2 cu yd
Concrete blocks	8" × 8" × 16"		110
Reinforcing steel	#4 rebar	20'	6
Dobie blocks	As needed	3"	
Brick	Common	2⅔" × 8"	576
Mortar			8 cu ft
Walls & misc			
Foundation sill	2×6 PT	12'	2
		8'	2
Joists & blocking	2×8 PT	8'	10
	2×8 PT	12'	3
Subfloor	⅝" AC or PTS T&G ply.	4×8	3
Studs & misc	2×4	8'	48
Top & sill plates	2×4	8'	6
		12'	6
Headers	4×8	10'	2
Sheathing	⅜" CDX ply.	4×8	10
Roof			
Rafters	2×6	8'	14
Blocking	2×6	12'	2
	1×6	8'	4
Outriggers	4×4	8'	2
Trusses	2×6	12'	1
(decorative)	4×4	8'	1
Collar ties	2×4	6'	5
Ridge board	1×8	14'	1
Sheathing	½" CDX ply.	4×8	7
Trim board	2×6	8'	4
	1×3	8'	6
Decorative ridge cap	2×6	14'	1
	2×2	14'	1
Drip edge	Galvanized	10'	7
Ridge flashing	10"	14'	1
Underlayment	30-lb felt		175 s.f.
Shingles	Fire-retardant wood shakes or equiv		175 s.f.

Materials List (continued)

Description	Material/Size	Dimension	Qty
Exterior finish			
Windows	Wood casement, divided lites	4'0" × 4'0"	3
Dutch door	Divided lites in upper	3'0" × 6'8"	1
Decorative trim	2×4 redwood	8'	26
Decorative beam ends	4×4	14'	1
Building paper	Type D		700 s.f.
Wire lath	Self-furring stucco lath		350 s.f.
Stucco moldings: bottom wall			40 l.f.
outside corner		8'	4
top wall			40 l.f.
Cement plaster	Premixed		350 s.f.
Stucco primer			2 gal.
Paint/stain			1 gal.
Interior finish			
Wallboard	½"	4×8	10
Flooring	Vinyl	12' width	8'
Wood baseboard			40 l.f.
Shelves, cabinets, desk			Varies
Hardware & misc			
Anchor bolts	½"	10"	16
Brick vents	Screened	8" × 16"	4
Joist hangers	2×8		14
Nails & screws	As needed		
Wall flashing (behind bricks)	Galvanized	12"	40 l.f.

Rake Board and Decorative Truss

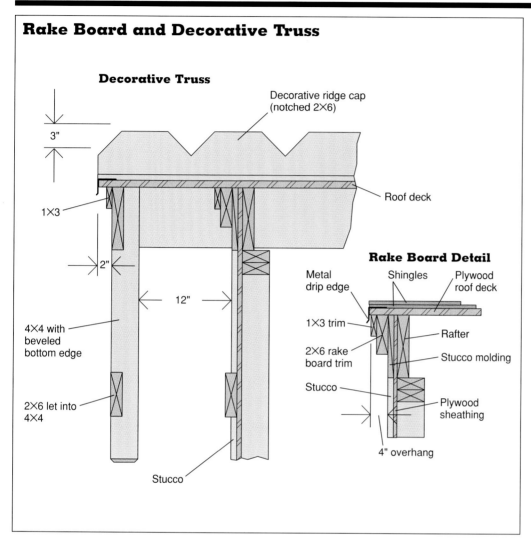

Decorative Truss

Decorative ridge cap (notched 2×6)

3"

Roof deck

1×3

2"

12"

4×4 with beveled bottom edge

2×6 let into 4×4

Stucco

Rake Board Detail

Metal drip edge

Shingles

Plywood roof deck

1×3 trim

Rafter

2×6 rake board trim

Stucco molding

Stucco

Plywood sheathing

4" overhang

Possible Interior Configuration

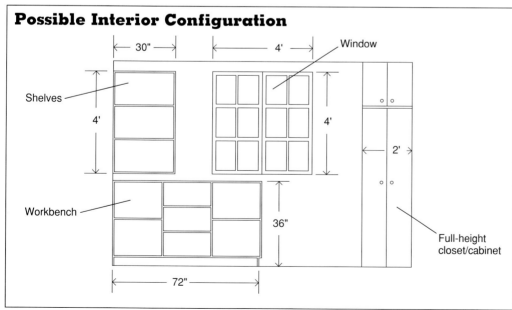

30"

4'

Window

Shelves

4'

4'

2'

Workbench

36"

Full-height closet/cabinet

72"

Build the decorative brick veneer up to the weep screed on the cement plaster. As you lay the courses, you'll need to add screen vents over the vent holes in the foundation.

Take your time. It helps to stretch a level string at the height where you want each brick to be in each course. Remember, it does not need to be absolutely perfect. As you finish each course, trowel off any excess mortar. If the brick looks spanking new, you might make a loose slurry to wash on the bricks to make them appear older.

Installing the Door

You can purchase an attractive prehung Dutch door. Install the jambs, shim them as necessary so the sides are plumb and the head is level, and hang the door. Install flashing over the top of the door opening before you apply the exterior trim.

Finishing the Interior

Under the window you can build a 36-inch-high cabinet or counter that can serve as a convenient work surface with open shelves beneath. When you install shelving on the adjacent walls, leave sufficient room to access the shelves under the counter.

If you plan to work in the cottage, consider laying sheet vinyl on the floor and finishing the walls with ½-inch wallboard and paint.

STORAGE COMPONENTS

This chapter presents ways to better utilize storage space: basic storage components that you can build yourself— shelves, racks, cabinets, hangers, and closets—from readily available materials. Most of these components work well to fit out the interior of a shed. Many can also be adapted to withstand outdoor conditions. The suggestions and designs presented here, along with "off the shelf" storage solutions that you can purchase, should provide the finishing touches to your customized storage system.

You don't have to be a cabinetmaker to outfit a shed for efficient and convenient storage. A few boards, some nails, and some common sense are all it takes to corral the clutter.

SHELVES AND CABINETS

The basic components of any storage system are shelves and cabinets. You probably have a few already, but it's likely that you can use more. Here you will find guidelines for building your own, which you can adapt to particular storage needs. In addition to being useful, attractive storage features may add value to your property.

Shelves

Probably the most common device for storage, shelves come in a wide range of shapes and sizes. The type you choose should be strong enough and big enough to accommodate whatever you need to store, and the shelves should be conveniently located: visibility and access are essential.

front edges of the shelves should be flush with the front edges of the uprights.

Turn the unit over so the back faces up. Make sure that the unit is square (check that the diagonal measurements are equal). Measure and cut the back piece so that its bottom edge covers the bottom shelf, and all other edges are inset ¼ inch from the out-

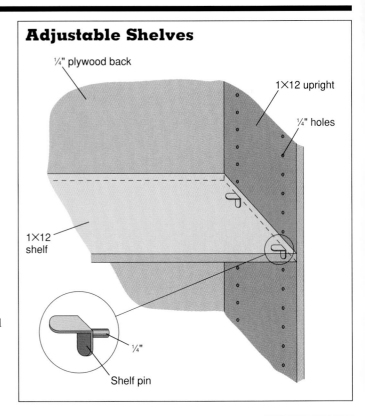

Adjustable Shelves

¼" plywood back

1×12 upright

¼" holes

1×12 shelf

¼"

Shelf pin

Plywood Shelf Unit

Two uprights, a few shelves, some nails, and glue are all it takes to make a strong and versatile shelf unit that's as easy to build as a box.

The 6-foot-tall unit shown at right can be built from a single sheet of ¾-inch plywood or five 6-foot 1×12s, plus a sheet of ⅛-inch or ¼-inch hardboard for the back.

Cut the uprights and shelves to length, then mark the shelf locations on the uprights. You can adapt the shelf spacing to your particular storage needs. Leave a 3½-inch space below the bottom shelf for a toe kick.

Assemble the unit on its back, gluing and nailing all of the shelves first to one upright, then to the other. The

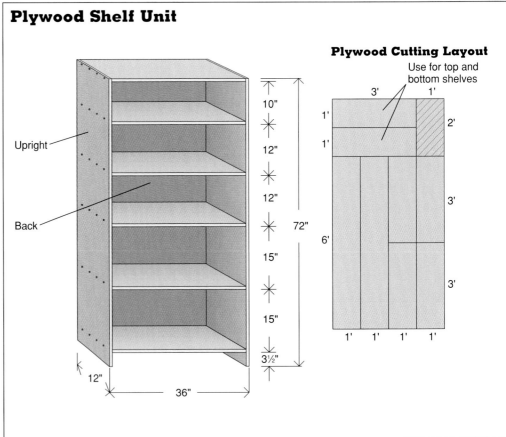

Plywood Shelf Unit

Upright

Back

10"
12"
12"
15"
15"
3½"
72"
12"
36"

Plywood Cutting Layout

Use for top and bottom shelves

3' 1'
1' 2'
1'
6' 3'
3'
1' 1' 1' 1'

side of the unit. Attach the back piece with glue and 1-inch by No. 6 wallboard screws or 6d box nails.

If you prefer adjustable shelves, attach only the top and bottom shelves as described. Then attach 2 strips of adjustable shelf track vertically on the inside of each upright, 1 inch from each edge, or drill rows of ¼-inch holes, 1 inch from each edge and 1 inch on center. These holes will accept ¼-inch dowels or shelf pins. To keep the holes aligned with one another, drill them in a long strip of scrap wood first, then use it as a jig to drill each row of holes in the shelf unit. Be sure not to drill all the way through the shelf uprights; use a drill stop.

Open Shelf Unit

This attractive and sturdy unit, 16 inches deep by 8 feet long, can handle virtually any normal storage load, including large, heavy items. Plywood shelves on 1×2 supports run the length and depth of the unit so that no span exceeds 32 inches.

Cut eight 2×2 uprights 6 feet long, eight 8-foot 1×2 stringers, and twenty-four 16-inch 1×2 cleats.

Cut ⅜-inch dadoes into the 2×2s for each cleat and stringer; cut corresponding ⅜-inch rabbets or dadoes into the cleats and stringers for the uprights. This will create a tight glue joint so that most of the weight rests on the up-

Lumber, Plywood, or Particleboard?

You may wonder which of these materials is best for building shelves and other storage units.

Wood boards are strong (very strong in the 2-inch thickness), have attractive edges, come in widths that usually do not require additional ripping, and are convenient to transport and store. However, they tend to cup and warp, and better grades can be very expensive.

Plywood is also strong and much more dimensionally stable than boards, due to the alternating grain orientation in each layer. It is rela-

tively inexpensive in shop grades and paint grades, which are suitable for garage and shed projects. The disadvantages are that full sheets are awkward to cut into shelving, and the edges of plywood shelves are not attractive unless they are trimmed with molding strips or edging.

Particleboard is weak and sags easily, even with very light loads; it is not suitable for shelves longer than 18 inches. Medium-density fiberboard (MDF), a cousin of particleboard used in cabinetmaking, is slightly stronger.

Open Shelf Unit

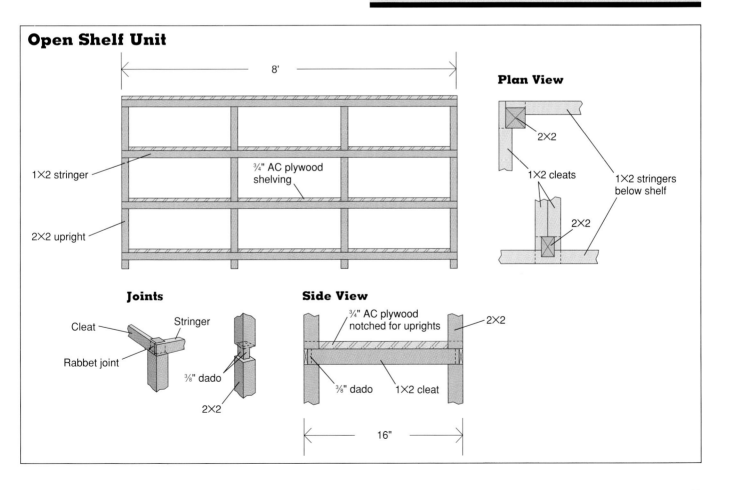

rights. The cleats will add to the strength of the shelf span.

Assemble the interlocking uprights and cleats, and glue and screw them together. Drill pilot holes to prevent cracking, and countersink the screws. Screw the frame to wall studs with 4-inch by No. 6 deck screws.

Next, cut ½-inch AC plywood shelves, with notches for the uprights. Glue and nail the shelves to the frame.

Shelves Between Studs

It is easy to overlook the storage potential of the space between studs. That extra 3½ inches of depth (for 2✕4 walls), added to every shelf you build, can create a significant amount of shelf space.

For shelves hung on knee braces or metal brackets, simply make the shelves 3½ inches deeper and cut slots for the studs into the rear of the shelves.

Alternatively, you could build minishelves between studs. The easiest are 2✕4 or 2✕6 blocks nailed between the studs with 16d sinker nails. Or you could nail 1✕1 cleats 3½ inches long to the sides of the studs and place ½-inch plywood or ¾-inch particleboard shelves on them.

Cabinets

Little more than boxes with doors, cabinets are the easiest way to store certain items. You may be able to recycle old kitchen cabinets or buy some ready built, but for the most

efficiency you will probably want to custom-build cabinets to fit the available space.

You don't have to be an experienced cabinetmaker to build the designs shown on these pages. Similar to kitchen cabinets but with less expensive materials and simpler joints, these cabinets use standard-sized lumber. They are a convenient height for people of average size, but you can adapt them. You may need to modify cabinet construction to fit the door style you prefer (see page 87).

Standard Lower Cabinet

Lower, or base, cabinets make excellent workbenches. Their dimensions, typically 36 inches high and 24 inches deep, provide a comfortable work height and ample, convenient storage space. Although they can stand alone, for stability you should anchor them to the floor or wall wherever possible.

For the top, bottom, ends, partitions, and shelves, use three 4✕8 sheets of ¾-inch plywood with at least one smooth side, such as Douglas fir AC plywood or paint-grade hardwood plywood.

First, rip one sheet in half the long way. Save one piece for the top and cut the other (the bottom) to 95 inches long.

Cut a 32-inch piece off one end of the second 4✕8 sheet and cut two 24-inch by 32-inch pieces out of it for the ends. Cut a ¾-inch rabbet, ¼ inch deep, along the bottom edge of each end piece.

Cut 3 partitions to 30½ inches high by 24 inches wide. Cut 8 shelves, 22⅞ inches long by 23 inches wide.

Next, lay out and drill parallel rows of ¼-inch-diameter holes, 1 inch on center, for adjustable shelf supports in the sides and partitions. To keep the holes aligned, make a jig (see page 83). Drill the holes all the way through the 3 partition pieces but not the ends.

Assemble the bottom and ends, with the pieces in position as if the cabinet were on its back. Join the pieces with wood glue and 1¼-inch by No. 6 wallboard screws.

Next, install the 3 partitions to create the 4 compartments; each compartment should be 23⁵⁄₁₆ inches wide.

After the glue sets, carefully turn the cabinet over on its face. Cut a 32-inch by 95½-inch back piece out of ¼-inch plywood and attach it with glue and wallboard screws. Tip the cabinet up and attach the top with glue and 8d finishing nails.

If you don't want to mar the top with nails, glue and screw 1✕1 cleats along the top of the ends and back before attaching the top. Then apply glue to the top edges of the cleats, ends, and partitions, lay the top in place, and drive screws up into the top through the cleats.

While the glue sets, fabricate a base out of 2✕4s or ¾-inch plywood. Cut 2 pieces 94½ inches long and 4 pieces 19 inches long (20½ inches, if you are using plywood). Glue and nail these together.

Then, apply glue to the top edges of the base. Place the cabinet on top so that it extends over the base front 2 inches for a toe kick. Nail or screw the bottom to the base.

Using Space Between Studs

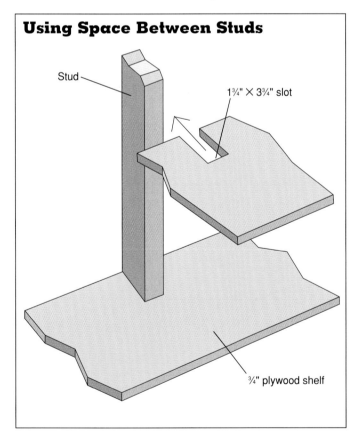

Stud

1¾" ✕ 3¾" slot

¾" plywood shelf

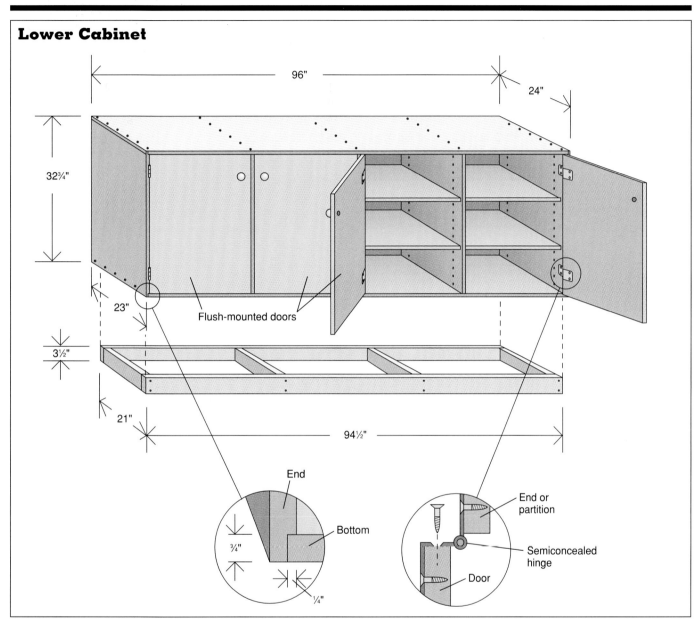

Lower Cabinet

96"

24"

32¾"

23"

Flush-mounted doors

3½"

21"

94½"

End

Bottom

¾"

¼"

End or partition

Semiconcealed hinge

Door

Move the cabinet in place against the wall. Using shims to keep the cabinet square, level, and plumb, screw the back to the studs. For door installation, see page 87.

Standard Upper Cabinet

For utilizing wall space above workbenches and countertops, upper cabinets are ideal. They are normally 11 to 12 inches

deep and are hung 18 inches above the countertop. The height of the cabinets can vary, but for maximum storage space and to eliminate potential dust catchers, you should build them to the ceiling.

Cut the top, bottom, and ends from 1×12s or from ¾-inch plywood. The pieces are all 11¼ inches wide. The top and bottom are 95¼ inches long; the ends are approxi-

mately 40 inches long, depending on ceiling height.

To provide a recess for the back piece, which is installed later, cut a ¼-inch-deep by ⅜-inch-wide rabbet into the back edge of each piece. Then, cut a ¾-inch rabbet, ⁷⁄₁₆ inch deep, along the inside top edge of each end piece. Cut a ¾-inch-deep by ⁷⁄₁₆-inch-wide dado ¾ inch up from the bottom. The dado will support the bottom

shelf, and the rabbet will strengthen the top joint.

Cut the shelves and partitions 11 inches wide. The 3 partitions are 37¾ inches long—or 2¼ inches shorter than the end pieces—and the shelves are 23⁷⁄₁₆ inches long. The shelves can be adjustable, as with the lower cabinet, or they can be fixed at roughly equal intervals. For fixed shelves, cut ¾-inch-wide by ⁷⁄₁₆-inch-deep dadoes in both

Upper Cabinet

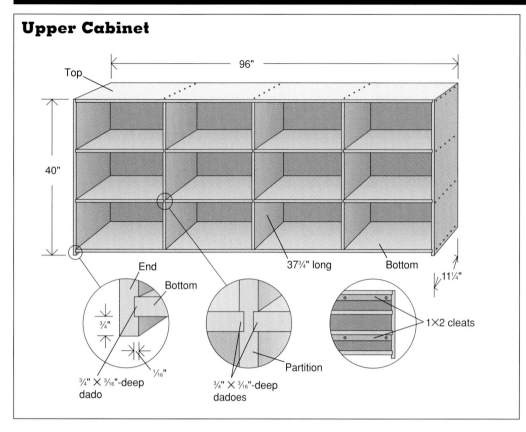

Top

96"

40"

End

Bottom

37¾" long

Bottom

11¼"

¾"

¾" × 3/16"-deep dado

1/16"

Partition

¾" × 3/16"-deep dadoes

1×2 cleats

Full-Height Cabinet

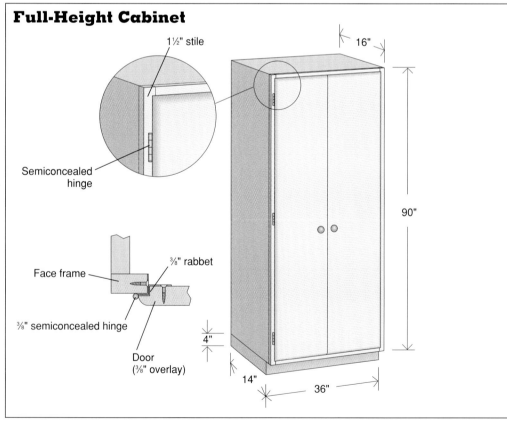

1½" stile

16"

Semiconcealed hinge

90"

Face frame

3/8" rabbet

3/8" semiconcealed hinge

Door (3/8" overlay)

4"

14"

36"

sides of the partitions and on the insides of the cabinet side pieces (see left).

Next, attach the top and bottom to the ends with glue and screws or, for a cleaner appearance, with glue and 6d finishing nails. Attach the back with glue and 4d box nails.

If the shelves are adjustable, glue and screw the partitions in place. If the shelves are fixed, attach the shelves of the 2 center sections to the partitions first and install the assembly in the cabinet as a unit. Install the end shelves in their dadoes by gluing them first and then toenailing them at the partitions and facenailing them at the ends.

Before hanging the cabinet, screw and glue 1×2 cleats to the back piece under the top and under the lower shelves. (If you have chosen adjustable shelves, attach the lower cleat above the bottom, on the inside, instead.) Hang the cabinet by screwing 2½-inch by No. 8 wallboard screws through the cleats into the wall studs. If there is wallboard, use 3½-inch screws.

Full-Height Cabinet

The construction for full-height cabinets is essentially the same as that for lower cabinets. Use ¾-inch plywood for the sides, top, bottom, and shelf; use ¼-inch plywood for the back. For the base, cut 4-inch strips of ¾-inch plywood.

Assemble the parts as shown at left. Install shelves or a clothes rod. If you need space for both, insert a plywood partition that will support shelves in one half and a rod in the other.

The door style suggested for this cabinet is a ⅜-inch overlay, but you could use either of the other styles described below.

Cabinet Doors

All cabinet doors are variations on 3 basic styles: flush, ⅜-inch overlay (also called half overlay or lipped), and full overlay. Each can be made from ¾-inch AC or paint-grade hardwood plywood.

Flush doors fit inside the cabinet openings. Because this leaves the edges of the cabinet partitions exposed, it is best to first cover the front of the cabinet with a face frame made from ¾-inch solid wood. You will have to adjust the cabinet dimensions accordingly. Or you could cover the exposed edges of the cabinet partitions with ¾-inch veneer tape.

A face frame is also required for ⅜-inch overlay doors. Full-overlay doors, which overlap the opening and cover cabinet edges, can be installed with or without a face frame. Each style requires a different type of hinge.

Face-Frame Construction

The stiles (vertical pieces) of most face frames are 1½ inches wide and extend the full height of the cabinet. The rails (horizontal pieces) are 1½ inches or 1¼ inches wide (although the bottom rail is often 1 inch wide); they fit between the stiles. You can nail and screw the frame pieces directly to the cabinet, but it is better to glue and dowel the stiles and rails together, then attach the entire frame to the cabinet as a unit.

Door Construction

Flush doors are easy to fabricate but require very precise measuring and cutting. Cut them from ¾-inch plywood to fit inside the cabinet openings, with a 1/16-inch gap all around. Attach a pair of semiconcealed (also called wraparound) butt hinges to each door by cutting a mortise in the door edge for clearance and screwing the hinges to the door backs. Hang them flush with the cabinet edges or face frame.

Less precision is needed to fabricate and hang ⅜-inch overlay doors, although they also require a face frame. Cut the doors ¾ inch larger than the opening in both dimensions. Then, cut or rout a ⅜-inch-deep by 7/16-inch-wide rabbet along all 4 edges (if 2 doors are paired, don't rabbet the edges where the doors meet). Hang the doors on the face frame with semiconcealed hinges that have a ⅜-inch inset.

Full-overlay doors, which cover all of the cabinet frame, are the easiest to build and hang. Cut the doors out of ¾-inch plywood. Each overlaps the opening enough to cover half the cabinet frame. Hang the doors on self-closing full-overlay, or European-style, hinges. Some hinges are installed by recessing them in round mortises cut into the door back; others are simply screwed to the cabinet and door surfaces. After installing the doors, adjust the hinges so that the doors hang evenly.

Workbench With Shelves

You can build a sturdy freestanding workbench using 2-by lumber. The workbench shown below measures 72 inches long, 36 inches high, and 24 inches wide.

Make a sturdy base out of 2×4s by attaching twelve 24-inch cleats to six 34½-inch legs with glue and 2½-inch deck screws. Make a top out of 2×6, 2×8, or 2×10 planks. Match the edges of the planks and join them with ½-inch dowels and glue, or attach several cleats across the bottom. Cleats are recommended if you don't want screw heads to show.

Center the top on the base and attach it with glue and 3-inch screws. If you don't want screw heads showing on the top, drive the screws diagonally through the cleats into the top from below.

Cut ¾-inch plywood shelves to fit over the lower cleats, then attach them with glue and 2-inch screws; they will stabilize the workbench and provide convenient storage for hand tools. If the bench needs additional reinforcement, attach it to wall studs, install diagonal bracing across the back, or attach ¼-inch plywood to the back.

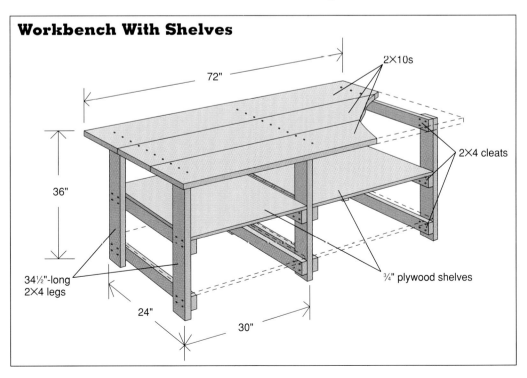

Workbench With Shelves

72"

2×10s

36"

2×4 cleats

34½"-long 2×4 legs

24"

30"

¾" plywood shelves

Hangers and Racks

If the floor of your garage or shed is cluttered with bulky lightweight items, you may be able to solve the problem by looking upward. One of the best ways to store such items is to use the ceiling and the walls.

Overhead Storage

You can use wasted overhead space by hanging items from beams, joists, or collar ties—as long as such framing members can bear the weight. The ideas suggested here are suitable for storing lightweight objects in most situations. For heavy loads you should consult with a structural engineer or other qualified professional. Some overhead framing members are designed only for reinforcing the roof structure and not for loads. Placing a concentrated heavy load in the wrong place could substantially weaken the entire roof system. When in doubt, ask an engineer.

Hanging Devices

Ropes can support items such as a kayak, a surfboard, pipe, or lumber. You can purchase polypropylene or sisal hemp rope, cable, hooks, or elastic ties from hardware and building-supply outlets. You can fabricate hooks from metal or knee braces from wood. The longer the object, the more ropes and loops you will need. Cushion smooth or fragile surfaces with rubber or carpet, and/or cover the rope with scraps of old garden hose. When you hang something, consider calling in a helper to give you a hand.

Plywood on Collar Ties

Collar ties, which hold rafters together, provide a storage area for lightweight, seldom-used items, such as empty boxes, holiday decorations, and camping gear. Typically, collar ties are installed on every other set of rafters; it's fine to install additional collar ties to create storage. As a rule of thumb, items that you can lift easily over your head will not overburden the ties.

You can store long objects directly on the ties, or make a simple platform out of ½-inch plywood with three 1✕3 braces attached lengthwise along the bottom to keep it from sagging.

Pipes and Rods

Of course, a clothes rod and some hangers serve to store work clothes, rain gear, winter coats, and similar items, but rods and pipes are also useful for storing other things. A pipe, for instance, works well for storing fan belts, extension cords, coils of rope, inner tubes, chains, hoses, and similar items; just lift one end to slip them over the pipe. For a large collection, use several short pipes instead of one long one, so you don't have to remove a lot of items to get to those in the middle.

You can hang pipes or rods anywhere you find supports for both ends: between 2 ceiling joists or collar ties, in a corner diagonally between the top plates, between 2 tall cabinets, or between a wall and a wire or chain hung from the ceiling.

Slings

A sling can support a shelf or individual objects. For a simple sling, screw or nail three 2✕4s together into a U shape. Tack one side to the ceiling joist, level the crosspiece, and attach the other upright to the joist with 5 screws. Then, secure the first upright with

Overhead Storage

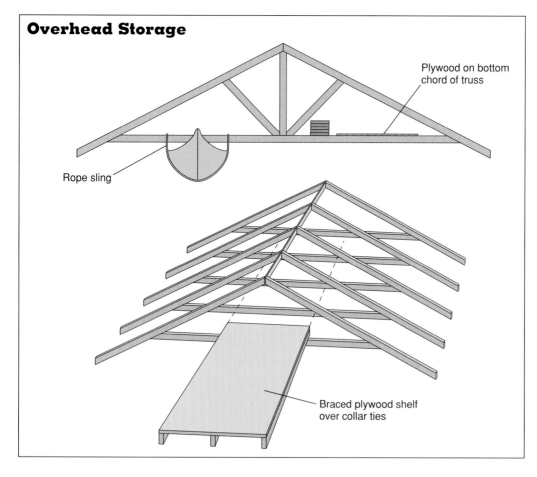

Plywood on bottom chord of truss

Rope sling

Braced plywood shelf over collar ties

Perforated Board in Frame

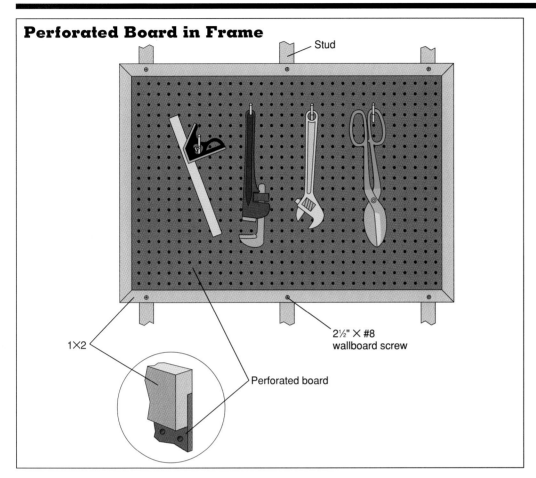

Stud

1×2

2½" × #8 wallboard screw

Perforated board

board on a flat surface, nail furring strips vertically along each wall stud and along the top and bottom of where the board will hang, using 8d or 10d nails. You can also make a frame of 1×2s, rabbeted to hold the board. Screw it to the studs with 2½-inch by No. 8 wallboard screws. To hang the tools, buy metal pegs and brackets, or use ⅛-inch dowels.

Specialized Racks

You can create special racks or storage spaces for virtually anything. Here are ideas for some items that commonly pose problems.

Bicycles

To store a bicycle in the least amount of floor area, suspend it from the wall by one wheel. This rack (see page 90) is easy to make and can be adapted to any size bike.

Glue and screw two 30-inch 1×6s to two 30-inch-long 2×2s. Screw these vertically to the wall, 2 inches apart, with the 2×2s on the outer sides.

Stand the bike on its rear wheel to establish the height of the brackets. Drill ½-inch holes on 1½-inch centers the length of both boards. Place the bicycle's front wheel between the 1×6s; holding the bicycle in place, slip a ⅜-inch pin through one hole, the wheel, and the corresponding hole in the other board. Slip a short wedge under the rear wheel to keep the wheel tight against the wall. To store 2 bicycles side by side, suspend the second one by its rear wheel.

5 screws and remove the tack. Hang a second sling on a nearby joist the same way.

Place a board across the slings for a convenient shelf, or store long objects directly on the slings. If you will be sliding objects on and off the slings frequently, brace them diagonally on each side.

Wall Racks

Vertical space can be maximized with wall racks. A sturdy rack can store a bicycle, wire, coils of rope, chain, or heavy tools. The most important considerations are that you should be able to reach objects without straining, and that the rack should be able to support whatever you decide.

Nails

The quickest rack is a nail in a stud. Normally, a 16d common nail is sufficient. If an item is heavy, use a bigger nail. You can hammer in a 20d nail, but for larger sizes, drill the stud so it won't split. You can also screw a 2×4 across several studs and hammer nails into it.

Dowels

Dowels can be used to hang items such as long-handled gardening tools. This is a convenient way to group tools. Screw an 8-foot 2×4 to the studs, then drill holes in the 2×4 for ½- or ¾-inch dowels, angling the tip of the drill downward and drilling

roughly 1 inch deep. Drill 2 holes for each tool, at least 2 inches apart, and space each pair of holes so that the tools will not overlap. Glue 4-inch-long dowels into the holes.

To fit more tools into less wall space, use a 5-foot-long by 3-foot-high piece of plywood instead of a 2×4. Lay the plywood on the floor, arrange the tools on it so that they nest in a compact pattern, and hammer nails or secure ½-inch dowels accordingly. Attach the plywood to the wall with lag screws.

Perforated Board

Numerous small items can be conveniently hung on perforated board. To mount the

89

Boats

Although you can suspend a small boat or canoe from the ceiling, it's safer to lean it against a wall or hang it from the wall. The primary concerns are to protect the sides of the boat and to prevent it from sliding or falling.

For a small open boat, build at least two (the number will vary with the length of the boat) 2×4 brackets as shown in the illustration below. Cut a rabbet in the vertical 2×4 to lap the horizontal one. Cut a rabbet in the horizontal 2×4. Join the 2×4s and nail the horizontal one to the stud and the soleplate with 12d nails. Tack scraps of thick carpet to each bracket to protect the boat.

Attach a cleat to the wall above the point where the boat will rest. Fasten a length of rope to the joint on each bracket. Hold the boat snug to the wall by securing the rope to the cleat.

Some boats can be stored resting on the stern, if you have sufficient vertical space. Using brackets similar to the ones shown, stand the boat on its stern and attach the bow line to a hook or ring that is securely mounted to the wall. To prevent chafing the line or scratching the boat, slip a scrap of old hose over the hook or ring.

Canoes are usually light enough to be hung from the wall. One method is with ropes run through 3 or 4 rings bolted to studs. You could also drill 1-inch holes through the studs to support sturdy pipes; hang rope slings from the pipes to hold the canoe.

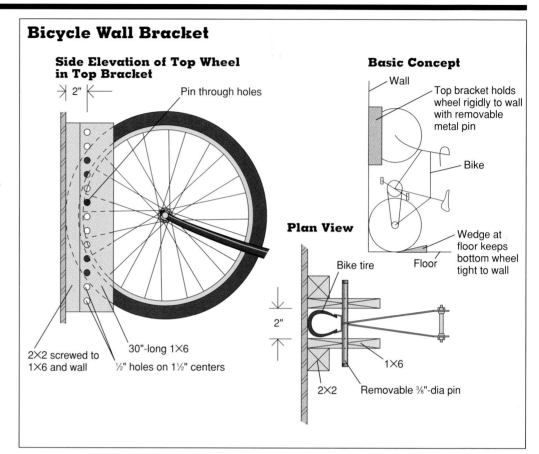

Bicycle Wall Bracket

Side Elevation of Top Wheel in Top Bracket

2"

Pin through holes

2×2 screwed to 1×6 and wall

30"-long 1×6

½" holes on 1½" centers

Basic Concept

Wall

Top bracket holds wheel rigidly to wall with removable metal pin

Bike

Wedge at floor keeps bottom wheel tight to wall

Floor

Plan View

Bike tire

2"

1×6

2×2

Removable ⅜"-dia pin

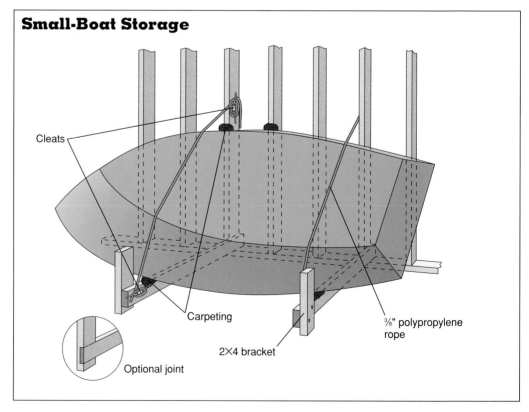

Small-Boat Storage

Cleats

Carpeting

2×4 bracket

⅜" polypropylene rope

Optional joint

Certain items remain outdoors for long periods of time because they belong there or because there is no room for them anywhere indoors. Lacking protection from sun, rain, and dirt, they deteriorate over time. Proper storage will keep them in good condition and improve the appearance of your yard.

Garden Hose Holders

You probably have a number of hoses connected to bibbs in various locations. The challenge is to store them neatly, so they remain in good condition and do not trip passersby, and at the same time are handy for use.

Although coiling a hose helps keep it neat, if the hose is on the ground it can get in the way and become dirty, and repeated coiling is tedious and time consuming. Here are some alternatives.

Pot or Bin for Coiling

Coil hose into a large terra cotta pot—some are made for this purpose—or construct a 3-foot by 3-foot bin with 2×10 redwood or pressure-treated lumber. This will hold not only the hose but also nozzles and sprinklers. Use ¾-inch plywood or 2×10 planks for the top. Use 2×4 cleats on the bottom to keep the bin above the ground. Drill at least four ¾-inch holes in the bottom of the bin for drainage.

Hose Hangers

A hanger keeps the hose off the ground and out of the way. To prevent the hose from kinking or tangling, rest it on a broad curved or angled surface.

Wood Hanger

If your hose is connected to a bibb on a short freestanding post in the yard, you can create a more convenient setup by sinking another, taller post in the same location. (This can replace the shorter post if you prefer.)

Make the post of 4×4 pressure-treated lumber or redwood, 4 to 6 feet long, and sink it at least 18 inches into the ground. Nail 2×4 knee braces (see below) to both sides of the post. Then, nail a shaped board or two—perhaps curves cut from a 1×12—to the tops of the knee braces to distribute the weight of the hose. Then, nail at least one board between the knee braces to prevent the hose from pulling them together.

If your hose bibb exits the house foundation or wall of the house, bolt a pressure-treated or redwood 2-by board to the wall and attach knee braces to that, or attach a 5-gallon plastic bucket horizontally to the board, using galvanized lag screws with washers through the bottom of the bucket. Coil the hose over the bucket, and store sprinklers or other small items inside it.

Metal Hanger

The most common store-bought hose hanger consists of heavy sheet metal with a curved surface on which you can coil the hose. Easy to install, it provides a quick solution to the hose-hanging problem.

An old tire rim makes an excellent homemade version. If you have one lying around, clean it up, paint it, and bolt it to a wall, a fence, or a post.

Hose Reel

Many garden and hardware shops sell hose reels. Some hang on a wall, some are free-standing holders with wheels, others have a sprinkler and move along the ground as you water the grass. You may prefer to purchase one of these. Or, with a little work and ingenuity, you might make the old tire rim described above rotate for use as a hose reel.

Hose Hangers

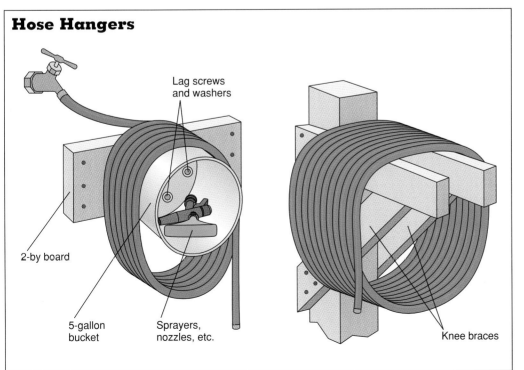

Lag screws and washers

2-by board

5-gallon bucket

Sprayers, nozzles, etc.

Knee braces

Building an Outdoor Closet

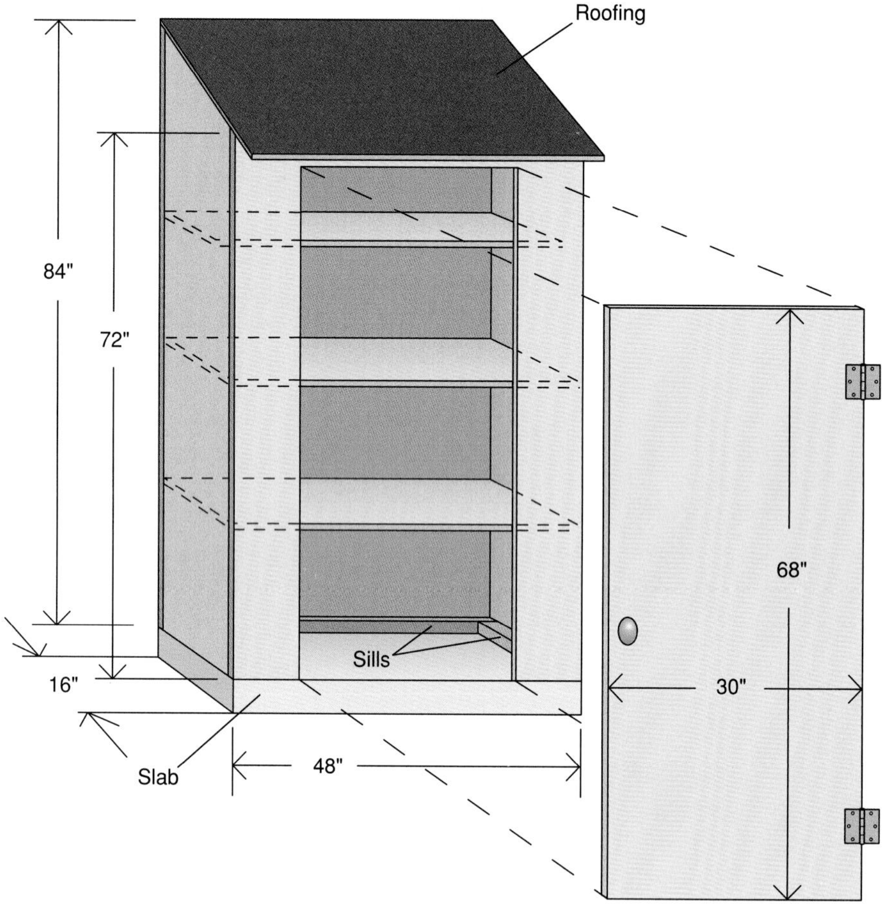

Roofing

84"

72"

16"

Sills

Slab

48"

68"

30"

Cutting Layout

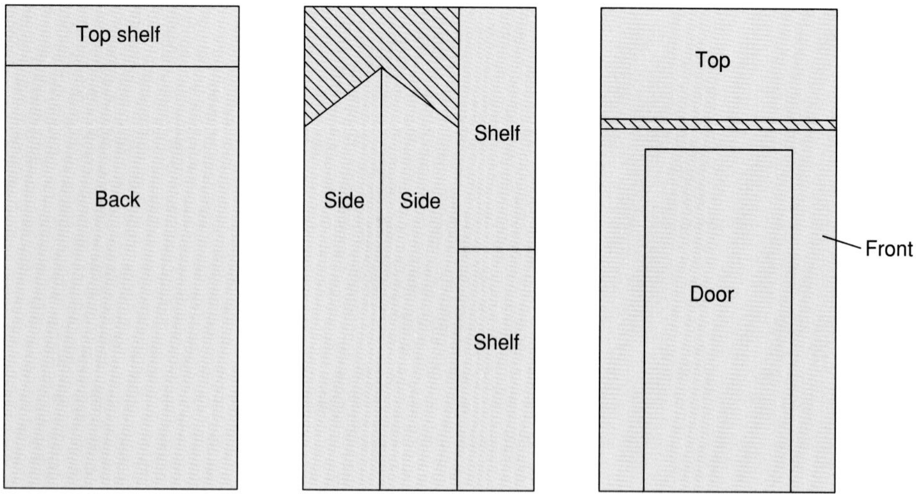

Top shelf

Back

Side Side

Shelf

Shelf

Top

Front

Door

Outdoor Closet or Cabinet

If your outdoor storage needs don't require a structure as large as the 6-foot by 12-foot Lean-to Potting Shed (see page 31), here are two less am-bitious alternatives. This out-door closet (16 inches by 48 inches) and outdoor cabinet (12 inches by 48 inches) are useful for storing items such as bicycles, grills, gardening tools, gloves, sprinklers, noz-zles, and containers for garbage and recyclables. You can build one or several clos-ets or cabinets right where you need them, usually against a wall or a fence where some protection from the weather is already available.

Outdoor Closet

The closet shown at left can be constructed out of 3 sheets of ⅝-inch CDX plywood. It can be freestanding or a lean-to. Stud walls or other framing are not necessary because the closet is only 16 inches deep and the shelves provide rigidi-ty. To ensure a dry floor, build it on a concrete slab, at least 4 inches thick, that measures 16 inches by 46½ inches. Attach pressure-treated 2✕4 sill plates around the edge of the slab (except in the door open-ing). An alternative would be to bolt the closet directly to a patio or deck where it will be protected from moisture.

Cut the plywood panels as shown at left. Using construc-tion adhesive and 8d HDG box nails, attach the 2 sides to the 3 large shelves at about 2-foot intervals. Attach the back, place the assembly in position

Outdoor Cabinet

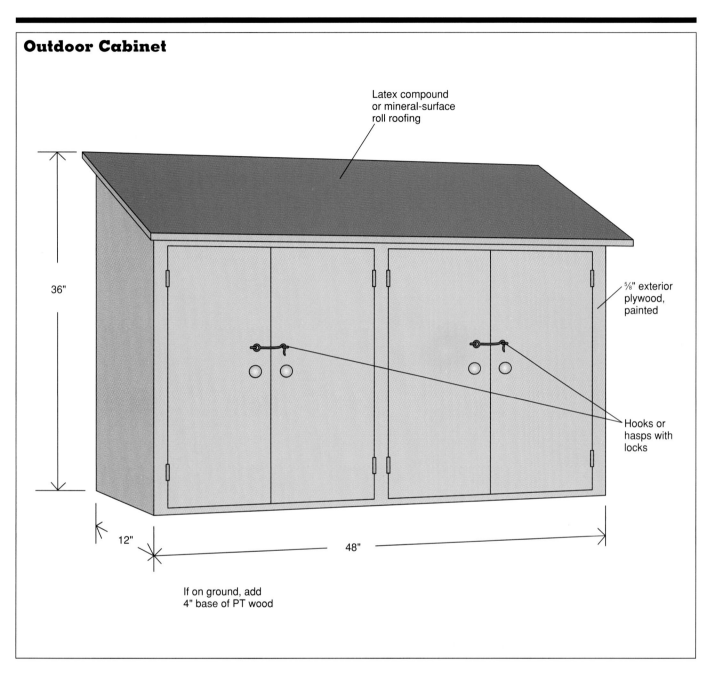

Latex compound or mineral-surface roll roofing

36"

⅝" exterior plywood, painted

Hooks or hasps with locks

12"

48"

If on ground, add 4" base of PT wood

on the slab, and attach the bottom of the sides and back to the 2×4 sill plates with 2-inch by No. 8 deck screws. Glue and screw the front in place, then the roof.

Nail metal drip edge along the sides and front of the roof, then cover the roof with mineral-surface roll roofing or latex decking surface compound. Attach hinges to the door and hang it. Add fascia or trim if you'd like, then paint the closet to match the house, add a door latch or hasp, and fill it with your outdoor treasures.

By adapting the overall dimensions and the shelf configuration of this closet, you can build similar closets for other items of differing sizes.

Outdoor Cabinet

Build an outdoor cabinet by using the same idea as the closet but on a smaller scale. This cabinet is 4 feet wide by 3 feet high, giving you 2 compartments and ample shelving. The sloped roof extends at least 3 inches beyond the front of the cabinet and 2 inches over the ends.

For the sides cut ⅝-inch CDX plywood 12 inches wide; attach a ½-inch plywood back. Use 1×2 cleats inside to attach the cabinet to the wall or a fence. Cover the roof with mineral-surface roll roofing or a latex roof sealant, then paint the cabinet.

INDEX

U.S./Metric Measure Conversion Chart

		Formulas for Exact Measures			Rounded Measures for Quick Reference		
	Symbol	When you know:	Multiply by:	To find:			
Mass **(weight)**	oz	ounces	28.35	grams	1 oz		= 30 g
	lb	pounds	0.45	kilograms	4 oz		= 115 g
	g	grams	0.035	ounces	8 oz		= 225 g
	kg	kilograms	2.2	pounds	16 oz	= 1 lb	= 450 g
					32 oz	= 2 lb	= 900 g
					36 oz	= 2¼ lb	= 1000 g (1 kg)
Volume	pt	pints	0.47	liters	1 c	= 8 oz	= 250 ml
	qt	quarts	0.95	liters	2 c (1 pt)	= 16 oz	= 500 ml
	gal	gallons	3.785	liters	4 c (1 qt)	= 32 oz	= 1 liter
	ml	milliliters	0.034	fluid ounces	4 qt (1 gal)	= 128 oz	= 3¾ liter
Length	in.	inches	2.54	centimeters	⅜ in.	= 1.0 cm	
	ft	feet	30.48	centimeters	1 in.	= 2.5 cm	
	yd	yards	0.9144	meters	2 in.	= 5.0 cm	
	mi	miles	1.609	kilometers	2½ in.	= 6.5 cm	
	km	kilometers	0.621	miles	12 in. (1 ft)	= 30.0 cm	
	m	meters	1.094	yards	1 yd	= 90.0 cm	
	cm	centimeters	0.39	inches	100 ft	= 30.0 m	
					1 mi	= 1.6 km	
Temperature	°F	Fahrenheit	⁵⁄₉ (after subtracting 32)	Celsius	32° F	= 0° C	
	°C	Celsius	⁹⁄₅ (then add 32)	Fahrenheit	68° F	= 20° C	
					212° F	= 100° C	
Area	in.²	square inches	6.452	square centimeters	1 in.²	= 6.5 cm²	
	ft²	square feet	929.0	square centimeters	1 ft²	= 930 cm²	
	yd²	square yards	8361.0	square centimeters	1 yd²	= 8360 cm²	
	a.	acres	0.4047	hectares	1 a.	= 4050 m²	